THE
HBCU
EXPERIENCE

THE SOUTHERN UNIVERSITY SYSTEM 3rd EDITION

Visionary Author: Dr. Ashley Little
Lead Author: Janea C. Jamison, MPA
Foreword Author: Dr. Derrick V. Warren
Foreword Author: LaQuitta A. Thomas, M.B.A

Published By: The HBCU Experience Movement, LLC

The HBCU Experience Movement, LLC

thehbcuexperiencemovement@gmail.com

Ordering Information:
Quantity Sales: Special discounts are available on quantity purchases by corporations, associations, and nonprofits. For details, contact the publisher at the address above.

ISBN: 979-8-218-25609-8

DR. ASHLEY LITTLE

A Message from the Founder
Dr. Ashley Little

Historically Black Colleges & Universities (HBCUs) were established to serve the educational needs of black Americans. During the time of their establishment, and many years afterward, blacks were generally denied admission to traditionally white institutions. Prior to The Civil War, there was no structured higher education system for black students. Public policy, and certain statutory provisions, prohibited the education of blacks in various parts of the nation. Today, HBCUs represent a vital component of American higher education.

The HBCU Experience Movement, LLC is a collection of stories from prominent alumni throughout the world, who share how their HBCU experience molded them into the people they are today. We are also investing financially into HBCUs throughout the country. Our goal is to create a global movement of prominent HBCU alumni throughout the nation to continue to share their stories each year, allowing us to give back to prestigious HBCUs annually.

We are proud to present to you *The HBCU Experience: The Southern University System 3rd Edition.* We would like to acknowledge and give a special thanks to our amazing lead author and expert author, Janea C. Jamison and Ayanna C. Spivey. Thank you both for your dedication and commitment. We appreciate both of you and thank you for your hard work and dedication on behalf of this project. We would also like to give a special thanks to our foreword authors, expert authors, contributing authors and partners of Southern University System for believing in this movement and investing your time, and monetary donations, to give back to your school. We appreciate all of the Southern University System alumni who shared your HBCU experience in this publication.

About Dr. Ashley Little

Dr. Ashley Little is Ms. Global Continental 2023 and the CEO/Founder of Ashley Little Enterprises, LLC, which encompasses her media, consulting work, writing, ghost writing, book publishing, book coaching, project management, magazine, public relations & marketing, and empowerment speaking. In addition, she is an award-winning serial entrepreneur, TV/radio host, TEDx speaker, international speaker, keynote speaker, media maven, journalist, writer, host, philanthropist, business coach, investor, advisor for She Wins Society, and 21-times award-winning bestselling author. As seen on Black Enterprise (2X), *Forbes* (2X), *Sheen* Magazine (Print and Online), Sheen Talk, Voyage ATL, Fox Soul TV, NBC, Fox, CBS, BlackNews.Com, Shoutout Miami, Shoutout Atlanta, Morning Star, Yahoo Finance, Heart and Soul, The Book of Sean, *HBCU Times*, *VIP Global Magazine*, The Black Report, Vocal, Ted.com, Medium, Soul Wealth, Hustle and Soul, BlackBusiness.com, Glambitious Top 21 Women Of 2021, New York Weekly's Top 10 Hardest Working CEOs alongside billionaire Mark Cuban, *US Insider's* Top 10 Women Entrepreneurs alongside billionaire and media mogul, Oprah Winfrey, *London Daily Post*, *Sheen* Magazine 5 Pioneers Making a Difference in Their Communities, NCA&T *Alumni Times*, CEO Weekly Top 10 Influential People in 2021 alongside billionaires Jeff Bezos and Beyonce' and many more. Through the Biden & Harris Administration, and Leaders Esteem Christian Bible University, she was also awarded with the Presidential Lifetime Achievement Award. She is a board member for Leaders Esteem Christian Bible University, as well.

As a recipient of the "Author of The Year" award by Glambitious, she is also a part of The Forbes Next 1000 Class of 2021 in partnership with Square. This first-of-its-kind initiative celebrates bold and inspiring entrepreneurs who are redefining what it means to run a business. Furthermore, she was a recipient of Nashville's Black 40 Under 40 Awards in December 2021. It is an annual event honoring the best and the brightest for their accomplishments in their chosen field and for their contributions and commitment to the African American community. Dr. Little is also an official member of For(bes) The Culture. For(bes) The Culture was formed in Boston at the Forbes Under 30 Summit in October of 2017. They pride themselves on convening current and future black and brown leaders worldwide to network, collaborate, share opportunities, and discuss issues related to their communities and the planet at-large. She was recognized along with other influential leaders and distinguished entrepreneurs, including Oprah Winfrey, Mel Robbins, Gary V and many more for the annual Brainz 500 Global Awards List awarded by *Brainz* Magazine. Lastly, she is a proud member of The Chancellor's Round Table at North Carolina A&T State University.

She is a proud member of Delta Sigma Theta Sorority, Incorporated, and a member of Alpha Phi Omega. She is very involved in her community, organizations and non-profits. Currently, she is the co-founder of Sweetheart Scholars non-profit organization, along with three other powerful women. This scholarship is given out annually to African American females from her hometown of Wadesboro, North Carolina who are attending college to help with their expenses. Dr. Little believes it takes a village to raise a child and she also encourages others to never forget where you come from. Dr. Little is a strong believer in giving back to her community. She believes our young ladies need vision, direction and strong mentorship. She is the CEO/Founder/Visionary Author of The HBCU Experience Movement, LLC, the first Black-owned company to launch books written and published by prominent alumni throughout the world who attended Historically Black Colleges & Universities (HBCUs). As authors, they share a powerful collection of stories on how their unique college experience has molded them into the people they are today. The purpose of The HBCU Experience Movement is to change the narrative by sharing Black stories and investing financially back into our HBCUs to increase young alumni giving and enrollment. The award-winning bestselling authors won the Black Authors Matter TV Award in May of 2021, Inaugural Anthem Awards of 2022, as well as the International Book Awards by The American Book Fest. The books are also part of the WorldCat.org, the world's largest network of library content and services. Dr. Little is also the Editor and Chief of *Creating Your Seat at The Table International Magazine*, advisor for She Wins Society, and writing and publishing coach for the WILDE Winner's Circle.

She is the founder and owner of T.A.L.K. Radio & TV Network, LLC, which airs in over 167 countries, and streams live on Facebook, YouTube, Twitter and Periscope. This broadcasting and media production company is for new or existing radio shows, television shows, or other electronic media outlets to air content from a centralized source. All news, information or music shared on this platform are solely the responsibility of the station/radio owner. She is also the owner and creator of Creative Broadcasting Radio Station, the station of "unlimited possibilities." She is also one of the hosts of the new TV Show *Daytime Drama* nationally syndicated television show, which will be aired on Comcast Channel 19 and AT&T Channel 99 in 19 middle Tennessee counties. It will also air on The United Broadcasting Network, The Damascus Roads Broadcasting Network, and Roku.

Dr. Little is a 17X award-winning bestselling author of, *Dear Fear, Volume 2: 18 Powerful Lessons of Living Your Best Life Outside of Fear*; *The Gyrlfriend Code, Volume 1*; *I Survived; Girl, Get Up and Win*; *Glambitious Guide to Being an Entrepreneur*; *The Price of Greatness*; *The Making of a Successful Business Woman*; and *Hello, Queen*. She is a co-host for The Tamie Collins Markee Radio Show, award-winning entrepreneur who is also a reflection contributor for the book, NC Girls Living in a Maryland World, Sales/Marketing/ Contributing Writer/Event Correspondent for *SwagHer Magazine*, contributing writer for MizCEO Magazine, contributing editor for *SheIs Magazine*, contributing writer/national sales executive for *Courageous Woman Magazine*, contributing writer for Upwords International Magazine (India), and contributing writer/global partner for Powerhouse Global International Magazine(London). Host of "Creating Your Seat At The Table", Host of "Authors On The Rise", Co-Host Glambitious Podcast, Partner/Visionary Author of The Gyrlfriend Code The Sorority Edition along with The Gyrlfriend Collective, LLC. Lastly, she has received awards, such as "Author of the Month"; The Executive Citation of Anne Arundel County, Maryland Award, which was awarded by the County Executive Steuart L. Pittman; and Top 28 Influential Business Pioneers for *K.I.S.H. Magazine* Spring 2019 Edition. She has been featured in *All About Inspire Magazine*, *Formidable Magazine*, *BRAG Magazine*, the front cover of MizCEO Magazine in November of 2019, the front cover for Upwords Magazine in the October 2019 Edition, *Courageous Woman* Special Speakers Edition in November 2019 and *Influence Magazine*. She has been featured on a nationally syndicated television show, *HBCU 101*, on Aspire TV, Dynasty of Dreamers *K.I.S.H. Magazine* Spring 2019 Edition, the front cover of *Courageous Magazine* in December of 2019, the front cover of Doz International Magazine in January 2020, Top 28 Influential Business Pioneers for *K.I.S.H. Magazine*, *Power20 Magazine Glambitious* January 2020 and *Power20 Magazine Glambitious* February 2020. She was also featured in *Powerhouse Global International London Magazine* March 2020 edition, *National Boss Magazine* in the October 2020 edition, *Sheen Magazine* February 2020 edition as one of "The Top 20 Women to Be on The Lookout for in 2020", BlackNews.com, BlackBusiness.com, the front cover of *She Speaks Magazine* August 2020 edition, as well as the front cover of *National Boss Magazine* November 2020 edition.

In addition, she's been featured on BlackNewsScoop.com, awarded the National Women's Empowerment Ministry "Young, Gifted & Black Award" in February 2020, which honors and celebrates women in business below age 40 for their creativity and business development. Featured in *National Women Empowerment Magazine, Black Enterprise,* as well as on Fox, NBC, and CBS, she was interviewed on *The Black Report* on Fox Soul TV and the front cover for *National Boss Magazine.* She was also a speaker at The Black College Expo 2020, for Creative CEOs Summit in January of 2021, and international speaker for Living Your Dream Life Summit 2021. She was also the speaker for the Elite Business Women Powershift Conference 2021, The Bella, The Brand & Her Bag Wealth Summit 2021, The Unstoppable You Summit in January 2021, the Marketing Mastery Summit for Glambitious 2021, the Crown Yourself Conference in January 2021, as well as the Door Dash Virtual Black History Month Celebration. As the speaker for Day of Aggie Generations with North Carolina A&T State University, Dr. Little was the 2021 Woman of Black Excellence Honoree, guest speaker on the podcast, The Happy Hour Show, speaker for the Phoenix Jack & Jill HBCU Author Showcase, as well as a guest on The JMosley Show. As contributing author for *Prayers for The Entrepreneurial Woman* book, she has spoken at Creative Con, been recognized as one of Today's Black History Makers, as well as being a featured speaker at From Paper to Profits Conference. She has been afforded the opportunity to gain press access for "Don't Waste Your Petty" movie as well as Mahalia Jackson's movie. She's been a speaker for HerStory Women's Global Empowerment Summit, HerStory Women Who Lead Conference, Stepping N2 Sisterhood Sharing Winning Secrets Virtual Summit, I AM Glambitious Virtual Conference, Black Authors Matter TV show, Thought Leaders Global Virtual Summit, as well as A Conversation with Floyd Marshall, Jr. As a Black Authors Matter TV award winner, she has spoken for Sheen Talk and served as the foreword author for the anthology *It Cost to Be the Boss.* Recognized by *VIP Global Magazine* as one of the Top 50 Most Influential Women, she has spoken at Black Writers Weekend, The GameChangers with Angela Ward Show, and served as keynote speaker for Blacks in Nonprofits Conference. Having served as speaker for the Leap

Conference, Pass the Mic Sis, the From Purpose to Profit Summit, and The Been Worthy Podcast, she has been the speaker and host for The MizCEO graduation, was featured in *Emoir Magazine* for Building a Global Media Empire, and was a Making Black History Today recipient for Glambitious.

Dr. Little received her undergraduate degree in English from North Carolina A&T State University. She received her master's degree in Industrial Organizational Psychology and her Doctorate in Leadership, as well. Dr. Little is a mover and shaker, and she continuously pushes herself to be better than she was yesterday. She gives God all the credit for everything that has happened in her life. She has strong faith and determination to be great. She believes her only competition is herself. Her favorite scripture is Philippians 4:13: "I can do all things through Christ who strengthens me."

Table of Contents

continued…

continued...

DR. DERRICK V. WARREN, D.B.A.

Foreword

Dr. Derrick V. Warren, D.B.A.
Associate Dean and Director of Graduate Programs
Southern University – Baton Rouge College of Business – SUBR '82 Computer Science

"By three methods we may learn wisdom:
First, by reflection, which is noblest; second, by imitation,
which is easiest; and third, by experience, which is the bitterest."

–CONFUCIUS

As an HBCU graduate and third year author of the HBCU Experience Movement Project - Southern University Edition, I want to focus this forward on technology exposure, education and experimentation. I am a computer scientist by degree. We are embarking on a new era of technological advancements, with artificial intelligence at the forefront. It is imperative that historically Black colleges and universities (HBCUs) are a significant player in shaping the future of this rapidly growing space. The importance of HBCU involvement in advancing technology must be prioritized. As an advocate for educational equity and a firm believer in the transformative power of knowledge, I want to use my story to encourage all readers to actively commit to pursuing knowledge in this domain.

Let us reflect on a few of these Science.Technology. Engineering.Math (STEM) Stars:

1. **Dr. Charles Drew** - Graduated from Howard University, Dr. Drew was a leading figure in the field of blood transfusion and developed a method for the long-term preservation of blood plasma.

2. **Dr. Gladys West** - A mathematics graduate from Virginia State University, Dr. West played a crucial role in the early development of the Global Positioning System (GPS).

3. **Dr. Reatha Clark King** - Graduating from Hampton University, Dr. King is a renowned chemist and executive who has held leadership positions in several scientific and research institutions.

4. **Dr. Jewel Plummer Cobb** - A biology graduate from Talladega College, Dr. Cobb was a prominent cancer researcher and the first African-American woman to lead a major university (California State University, Fullerton).

5. **Dr. Mark Dean** - Graduated from Tennessee State University, Dr. Dean is a computer scientist who played a key role in the development of the IBM personal computer and is credited with many significant advancements in computer hardware.

6. **Dr. Walter S. McAfee** - Graduated from Howard University, Dr. McAfee was a mathematician and physicist who made significant contributions to the field of telecommunications and radar technology.

7. **Dr. Sandra Johnson** - A graduate of Southern University and A&M College, Dr. Johnson is a Master Inventor and the first African American woman to earn a Ph.D. in Electrical and Computer Engineering in the United States. Dr. Johnson also worked on the prototype of the SP2 processor for IBM's "Deep Blue" chess machine, as well as other technology areas.

Black colleges and their graduates have been at the forefront of nurturing intellectual curiosity and innovation since being established in the 1800's. Our institutions have consistently produced exceptional graduates who have made significant contributions to various sectors. However, despite our rich legacy, HBCUs have been underrepresented in the Science, Technology, Engineering and Math (STEM) fields.

This is not a reflection of the talent, skill base and potential within HBCUs, but rather a long history of systemic inequities, barriers and disparities. With the recent Supreme Court decision that removes race as a consideration for college admissions, the focus on ensuring diversity on our college campuses with our universities (HBCUs and others). This decision could also have impacts in all aspects of the corporate and industrial environment.

Furthermore, HBCUs have a profound understanding of the challenges faced by marginalized communities. By incorporating and prioritizing a social justice lens, HBCUs can contribute to the development of technology that caters to the needs of underserved populations. This approach ensures that the advancements in technology are not only inclusive but also considerate of the diverse perspectives and experiences within our society.

HBCUs can also serve as platforms for technological innovation and entrepreneurship. By fostering a culture of innovation and providing opportunities for students to translate their ideas into tangible products or services, HBCUs can play a vital role in creating a vibrant technological ecosystem. This not only drives economic growth but also empowers our students to become agents of change and leaders in the field of technology.

As I conclude my foreword, I want to restate that HBCU involvement in advancing technology must be continuously encouraged. By seizing this opportunity, we can shape a future that is inclusive, equitable, and driven by the values of diversity and social justice. The world is missing our stories and it is up to us to tell them. STEM stories. Art stories. Education stories. Sports stories. Entertainment stories. Music stories. Love stories. War stories. Dance stories. History stories. Life stories. So many stories. Let us continue to tell our stories.

In the prolific words of Toni Morrison, we must continue to *"Write the story the world is missing"*.

About Dr. Derrick V. Warren, D.B.A.

Growing up in a small town, Bastrop, La., taught Derrick the importance of relationships, results and resilience.

From a young age, his parents, Calvin and Idell Warren (both HBCU graduates), instilled in him the reality that a quality education is extremely important for success. "Education is a great equalizer in a world that is not always fair", states Dr. Warren. Now, this self-described "Global Life Learner" drives positive transformation for the Southern University System (SUS) through multiple roles including Associate Dean and Director of Graduate Programs for the Southern University Baton Rouge College of Business, past Director of Alumni Affairs, and International Business Machines (IBM) – SUS Single Point of Contact (SPOC) for IBM Global University Programs. In his role as IBM – SUS SPOC, Dr. Warren leads the implementation of the IBM Academic Initiative, IBM Academic Awards and IBM Skills Academy programs for the university system. This powerful partnership provides technology, research opportunities, and grants and supports the advancement and acceleration of in demand skills such as Artificial Intelligence, Blockchain, Cloud, Cybersecurity, Data Science, Design Thinking, Internet of Things and Quantum Computing for students, faculty and key stakeholders of the university. He performs these critical tasks by utilizing social/digital engagement, technology transformation, strong communication strategies and innovation.

Prior to his roles with Southern, Dr. Warren spent over 32 years with IBM and was responsible for the overall client satisfaction, financials, and delivery execution of large accounts ranging in size from several hundred million to over a billion dollars in total contract value. While at "Big Blue" Warren achieved success living abroad leading teams that provided complex technology solutions for corporations in Asia Pacific and Africa. He also developed compelling value propositions, created innovative tactical/strategic plans, executed roadmaps for effective execution, resolved complex escalated issues/disputes as well as guided the participation of all IBM Lines of Business. He has also published articles in industry magazines and is an accomplished speaker at business symposiums, conferences, and universities around the world.

Warren is a cum laude honor graduate of Southern University in Baton Rouge, LA, with a Bachelor of Science degree in computer science. He earned an MBA from the University of South Florida in Tampa, and his Doctorate in Business Administration from Georgia State University – Robinson College of Business in Atlanta, Georgia. Dr. Warren is certified in Online Teaching from Quality Matters, has his Master Teaching Certificate from Georgia State, Blockchain Technologies certification from the Massachusetts Institute of Technology (MIT) Diversity, Equity and Inclusion certificate from the University of South Florida and a Careers in Real Estate Certificate from the University of Alabama.

He and his wife (college sweetheart), Anita, currently reside in Baton Rouge, La. They are the proud parents of two sons, the late Derrick II and Dillon; daughter, Dhalyn; and granddaughter Emersyn.

LAQUITTA A. THOMAS, M.B.A.

Foreword
LaQuitta A. Thomas, M.B.A.
Southern University and A&M College – Class of 1993
President Emerita – Southern University Alumni Federation

The Southern University System…
it's a brand, it's our HBCU brand!

Picture it…it's the fall and the setting is A.W. Mumford Stadium on the 512-acre campus known as Southern University and A&M College, The Bluff. It's been a beautiful sunny day full of great food, big fun and major fellowship, where Southernites have barbecued, boiled and fried their favorite Louisiana cuisine in anticipation for the thousands who will take over 'the yard'. It's six o'clock in the evening and the stadium lights are illuminated and the venue is packed with students, alumni, administrators, faculty, spectators, fans, the Southern University cheerleaders, the 250+ member Southern University "Human Jukebox" Marching Band, LaCumba, the Southern University mascot and, last, but not least, the Southern University Jaguar football team. Everyone you see has on some variation of Southern University gear, ranging from columbia to navy blue and gold, and most, are "SU down" from head to toe, literally! The Southern University Jaguars score moments before the half-time buzzer sending the stadium into a frenzy and it's so loud, that our Scotlandville neighbors can hear the cheers and screams coming from across 'The Hump'. The Southern University "Human Jukebox" Marching Band has already taken over the sidelines in preparation for an invigorating and highly anticipated half-time show. Thus, leaving all of the aforementioned individuals to take the lead on singing the Southern University Fight Song.

It's in that single moment, those who represent the Southern University System, across the globe (because we are international), are all on the same page. It's in that single moment, those who represent the Southern University System all agree and are aligned on the greatness of our University System. It's in that single moment, Southernites, in-person and those listening and watching on their favorite devices, all recognize the excellence, pride and tradition of the Southern University brand, and that it's **our** HBCU brand. It's at that moment, that no matter when or if you 'walked the yard', Southernites are all collectively cheering for the brand that is Southern University.

As the Southern University "Human Jukebox" Marching Band 'takes the field', we hear The Voice himself, Mr. Darrin Bedell exclaim boldly and proudly "It is the S on the chest that lets you know that they're the best." That's the Southern University brand and every week of our football season, the Human Jukebox reminds us that our HBCU experience is the best!

It wasn't until I was older and spent some years in my corporate career, that I recognized the Southern University System is an entire brand and that branding matters. After sitting in work meetings with marketing minded individuals, I began to earnestly reflect on the Southern University System HBCU experience and really invest time in determining what our brand meant to me. As someone who truly loves 'all things Southern', I embraced factors about our brand that didn't always resonate positively and this sent me into problem solving mode. My thoughts quickly moved to approach and implementation and how we can render a better result for our brand! I still think like that to this very day and in my moments of reflection, there is a genuine thought around what my SU brand says about me and my commitment to the Southern University System.

In this amazing edition of The HBCU Experience – The Southern University System, you will read detailed, honest and authentic stories from Southernites, who represent the Southern University System brand. It's in this collection of HBCU experiences, that another moment in time is captured and documented where, like in a successful stakeholder meeting, alignment is attained on just how impactful the Southern University experience has been and is. Each of these authors share their journey and provide a picturesque account of why Southern University was their choice and why Southern University is still their choice! These writers share what's in their hearts about their favorite HBCU and, that after God and their mothers, Southern University is next!

After 143 years of existing, the Southern University System brand continues to shine brightly and provide growth and opportunities. Our students graduate and have endured the readiness needed to solve the problems presented in this global economy. Our alumni represent the Southern University System brand globally and in many different industries. Just as the brick and mortar on our five campuses represent the brand, our students, alumni, faculty and staff are the face of the Southern University System and must be the gatekeepers. Just like those individuals at A.W. Mumford stadium, we have to stand courageously and recognize how empowered we are because of what we know our HBCU brand to be. Our HBCU brand matters! As we continue to grow and evolve, the Southern University brand should become personal to all of us as Southernites. What does your SU brand say about you and your commitment to the Southern University System? Make your HBCU experience and brand personal.

Thank you, Dr. Ashley Little, for shining the spotlight on my favorite HBCU and the only HBCU system that exists!
We appreciate you for providing this platform for so many to share their Southern University experience and to showcase the Southern University System brand!

About LaQuitta A. Thomas, M.B.A.

LaQuitta Thomas works as an Information Technology Project Manager and certified Agile ScrumMaster with Texas Instruments, Incorporated in Dallas, Texas, and has been with the company for 29 years. LaQuitta is very active in the areas of Engineering and IT recruitment and talent development at Texas Instruments and was appointed campus champion for TI at Southern University and A&M College in 2003, and in 2007 as Executive Sponsor. During LaQuitta's tenure as Executive Sponsor, Texas Instruments donated $750,000 to support student scholarships, the TI Automated Test Engineering class and student organizations in the College of Sciences and Engineering.

LaQuitta was educated in STEM (Science, Technology, Engineering, Math), having earned a Bachelor of Science degree in Mathematics with a minor in Computer Science from The Southern University and A&M College in Baton Rouge, Louisiana in December 1993. She earned a Master of Business Administration specializing in eCommerce from the University of Dallas Graduate School of Management in 2001.

LaQuitta is a Life member of the National Black MBA Association and in December of 2018, was named the organization's Community Champion of the year. She is committed to STEM and serves the National Society of Black Engineers and is a Life member of the Beta Gamma Sigma Honor Society.

LaQuitta is afforded many opportunities to give back to the community as a Diamond Life member of Delta Sigma Theta Sorority, Incorporated. She celebrated 25 years of service in the sorority in 2019.

LaQuitta supported diabetes research for 20 years in the Dallas-Fort Worth area with the Juvenile Diabetes Research Foundation and served on the Corporate Advisory Council for the Sickle Cell Disease Association of America.

In 2018, LaQuitta was inducted into the National African American Women's Leadership Institute (NAAWLI) and partnered with a colleague on developing "STEMage Is Everything", a concept that encourages young ladies to see and create their identity in STEM. As a result, LaQuitta now serves on the North Dallas High School Advisory board working with the administration, faculty and students on career readiness and promoting STEM.

LaQuitta was selected in March 2019 as a "Hidden Figure – Top STEM Influencer" in the DallasFort Worth area by the National Society of Black Engineers, an honor she cherishes.

LaQuitta is passionate about assisting our next generation of leaders and their transition from the dorm room to the board room and spends time mentoring college students and new college grads on career planning and chartering their professional and personal roadmap. LaQuitta, who has mentored and advised countless students over the years, created a career bootcamp 101 workshop. The workshop is designed to assist college students with preparing for and landing great careers after graduation. She enjoys sharing career leading practices with college students and has conducted the bootcamp workshop at HBCUs Morehouse College, Spelman College and Southern University and A&M College.

As part of LaQuitta's commitment to education, she created the IgNite InSpire STEM scholarship. The scholarship will be awarded in 2023 to one female student at all 5 of the Southern University System campuses and is designed to ignite, inspire and celebrate young women in the Southern University System majoring in a STEM discipline.

LaQuitta is an extremely proud and active member of The Southern University Alumni Federation and was elected as the first female National President of the 82-year old organization July, 2018 and National President Emerita, July 2022. She was honored and humbled to serve as the 19th National President for the SU Alumni Federation and continues to be committed to increasing Alumni engagement, SU Support, helping Southern re-establish national academic prominence and building relationships with more corporate partners to benefit the SU System. LaQuitta is over the moon excited to continue giving back to the SU System and the students!

LaQuitta, a true servant leader, is dedicated to impacting the next generation with education, career and professional development opportunities. She firmly believes in the scriptures "your gift will make room for you" and "to whom much is given, much is required". She's enthusiastic, energized and excited about the road ahead and believes the best is yet to come.

JANEA C. JAMISON, M.P.A.

O, to be a Jaguar: The Next Chapter
Janea C. Jamison, M.P.A.

"O, to be a Jaguar! You know, legend has it that God must be a Jaguar... that's why He made the sky blue and the sun gold."
–A SOUTHERN UNIVERSITY ALUMNI

Welcome to My Chapter

I am Janea Jamison, a small-town lady with esteemed dreams. Writing as the lead author of the Southern University System Edition of the HBCU Experience Movement has been an honor for the past three years.

As with everything, my journey has changed and altered, and my dreams have continued to elevate and expand. However, as I think of my successes and accomplishments throughout the years, I would be remiss if I did not share the institution, experiences, and opportunities that have propelled me into the beautiful life I have and the woman I am today. My life would be nothing without my commitment to honoring God, serving the community, and my connection to Southern University. I often say "I am Southern University," "I bleed blue and gold," and "I am the Bayou Classic." Although I say these things jokingly, the values aligned with the university and its commitment and values to tradition stem deep within my overall well-being.

God, Community (family), and Southern University will be a part of me forever. Now, let me share with you how I discovered this revelation of what matters the most to me, and how these three entities keep me rooted and grounded.

My Journey to SU

I grew up in a rural country town just 45 minutes outside of Baton Rouge, Louisiana. However, the demographics and culture differed entirely from Baton Rouge. A typical day after school involved dance team practice or fishing along Bayou Lafourche. My favorite meals then were rabbit, white beans, rice, and alligator sauce piquant. I loved attending mass, listening to blues with my "Daddie," being babied by my aunts, and surrounding myself with my cousins, who were more like sisters. My mom and I also shared an unbreakable bond throughout my childhood. I was my mother's "shadow" and didn't experience life without her–I loved my family, community, and catholic upbringing. They were my foundation and shaped me into who I was throughout my adolescent years, but, little did I know, Southern University would profoundly impact my life and revolutionize my vision and life experiences to a whole other level.

The spring semester before High School graduation, I anxiously awaited my acceptance to Southern University. I applied to a few schools, but SU was the only college I looked forward to attending. My first SU experience was "Jaguar Preview." Jaguar Preview was freshman orientation the summer before the fall semester.

Although I am outgoing, this "new" experience caused me to be shy, nervous, and afraid to start over. My high school classmates would attend PWIs or other great HBCUs like Xavier University.

New beginnings are rough.

Oddly enough, I feared entering a world other than the catholic school education I'd embraced for the past fifteen years. Would others accept my quirkiness and music choices? I was unsure how to cope in an environment different from my childhood and upbringing.

Yet, here I was, a young Catholic schoolgirl from the deep, rural south, ready to take on Southern University. I was fortunate enough to make solid friendships from Jaguar Preview that would last a lifetime. The entire summer, we remained in contact and planned to room together on campus in the fall. Anticipation grew deep in August of 2008, the start of my first semester. Before our official move-in day on campus, my friends and I met at the McDonald's at the corner of Scenic Highway and Harding Boulevard, right outside campus, "across the hump." We fellowshipped with our parents, ready to take on Southern University and move into S.V. Totty Hall. In my eyes, the campus was *huge*! It was filled with promising young students who looked like me but came from various cultures and backgrounds. I was so eager to have my "A Different World" experience.

JAGS for Jamison

A familiar face welcomed me to SU as I stood in line, waiting for my dorm room number. I was so excited to see someone I had known before freshman orientation. She, at the time, was a senior, and she wasn't just any senior; she was 'Miss Senior' and served on the Royal Court.

Miss Senior and I had a similar background, attending the same private high school and having a small rural upbringing. I was thrilled to see a familiar face. Once I settled in and adjusted to campus life and friends, the current Miss Senior encouraged me to run for Miss Freshman.

She encouraged me to step out on faith and embrace the unknown, which was the very same thing I feared.

I didn't want to disappoint Miss Senior, but I was uncertain if I would be a good face for my class. Again, would people like me? How much time and effort would running my first SGA campaign take? However, I didn't allow those uncertainties to stop me. Those thoughts resonated with me and motivated me to embark on a new journey: Miss Freshman 2008-2009, and the 'JAGS for JAMISON' campaign began.

I had about $500 of unused scholarship funds. The encouragement from Miss Senior and my mother allowed me to lead my first successful SGA campaign. I used my platform as Miss Freshman to vocalize students' concerns to the board, host beautification projects around campus, and assist Miss Southern University with her St. Jude Children's Hospital initiatives. Being Miss Freshman taught me to step outside of the box. It taught me never to be afraid to try new things simply because I didn't know the outcome. It also allowed me to broaden my network within the Southern University system as I met students at SUNO and SUSLA. That spring semester, I even had my first campus job. I worked at the Southern University Ag Center. I also learned the importance of sharing my experiences early in my first year. I signed on as an SU Student Ambassador, gave tours to high school students, and expressed my joy as a Southern University student. As a political science major, I even registered students to vote and organized students to the state capitol to protest against budget cuts.

That summer, I embarked on my first political job and served under the mayor of my hometown. I wanted to understand why my campus was beautiful, but the neighborhood surrounding my beloved institution encompassed a proliferation of dollar stores and fast food restaurants; it was essentially a 'food desert.' I learned the systems of parish government, local judiciary systems, and how to draft and implement local policies. I used these skill sets to spark others to raise similar concerns, so we could collectively build and strategize on implementing change. Being active on campus and utilizing my voice prepared me for my career. I saw the importance and value of speaking up and speaking out. My involvement with SGA, organizing, and politics also pushed me to question those in positions of power. There was so much fulfillment in working for causes much greater than myself.

With that said, I longed to be connected to one of the greatest organizations on campus, the FIRST of its kind—Alpha Kappa Alpha

Sorority, Incorporated. As a child, I was introduced to this illustrious sisterhood by attending regional conventions and boules with my great aunts. All the fears of acceptance by others rose again when I sought interest in joining AKA. Am I good enough? Would members embrace me? The journey was arduous. I questioned myself and my capabilities but made it through the 'burning sands.' On Sunday, November 8, 2009, I became an initiate of THE Beta Psi Chapter of Alpha Kappa Alpha Sorority, Inc. AKA broadened my leadership capabilities. I grew an even deeper love for community engagement and helping others. As I led my organization, I also ushered in the 'streets' by doing good, seeking justice, and volunteering to work on political campaigns. I vowed to support candidates who shared my values and wanted to change the poor infrastructure and leadership throughout the state. I completed my undergraduate studies in May 2012, graduating Cum Laude with a 3.7 cumulative GPA, the second highest in my department. I continued to build my political career and served as a legislative assistant to a City Council member, and furthered my education. I received my Master's in Public Administration in December 2015. I knew that, with GOD, all things are possible, and He would continue to give me clarity within my journey of serving the community. It was also clear that my Southern University network of professors and counselors are family. My SU family sealed the glue between my network and leveraging my career, providing me with sound advice and connections. It was clear that my friends turned family. My campus interests turned into passions, and my experiences molded me to aim for the stars. So again, it is through God, Community, and Southern University, I have accomplished what I have today.

Legacy

As a 2012 and 2015 Southern University and A & M College graduate, my HBCU experience allowed me to find my voice and passion within policy and advocacy.

In 2022, at 32 years old, I was sworn in as a federal appointee to serve as the Regional 6 Advocate within the Biden-Harris Administration within the US Small Business Administration-Office of Advocacy. In this role, I represent the interests of small businesses in the western United States by collaborating with business owners, state and local governments, and business associations–and advocating on their behalf at Capitol Hill and throughout the federal government.

I've also built a career focusing on organizational growth and programs advancing voting rights, uplifting women of color in leadership positions, and supporting Black men and boys. My growth in policy, advocacy, diversity, and racial equity work is rooted in the experiences shared throughout college and the global network built in furthering my career. My HBCU experience taught me to trust in God, work hard, never forget the community, and work to build a better future for tomorrow. I will always hold Southern University and my friendships near and dear to my heart. I cannot wait until my next chapter continues to grow, and I can further build on my legacy.

Thank you, Southern University; I owe my all to Thee!

About Janea C. Jamison, M.P.A.

Policy Advocate, Bestselling Author, Social Impact Strategist

Janea Jamison is a longtime advocate for race and gender justice. Janea is a Louisiana native and hosts a weekly podcast called *Her Story, L.L.C.* She creates opportunities for critical dialogue and action for Black Women who have defied obstacles and turned them into success. Her justice lens focuses on centering BIPOC women and girls in policy, organizing, and advocacy to develop a roadmap for equity.

In September 2022, Janea was appointed by the Office of Advocacy to serve as the Regional Advocate for Region 6 within the U.S. Small Business Administration, where she works with small business owners, state and local governments, and small business associations to bring the voice of Region 6 to Washington DC.

Prior to her appointment, Janea led all programming strategies for the Power Coalition. Her work included:

- The statewide growth of the Power Coalition and the implementation of core programming, including She Leads— a leadership program for female leaders of color.

- Black Men and Boys Statewide work.

- Voting rights work.

- Policy/advocacy work.

Under Janea's leadership, the Power Coalition led a successful 2020 statewide Census campaign that utilized a digitally informed approach to reach thousands of "Hard to Count" Louisianians across the state during a pandemic. She led a comprehensive Election Protection Program in partnership with NAACP Legal Defense and Educational Fund and The Lawyers' Committee for Civil Rights

Under Law. Before her position with the Power Coalition, Janea worked with the East Baton Rouge Metro Council as the Legislative Assistant to Councilwoman Erika L. Green (D-5) and Court System Supervisor in Assumption Parish under the leadership of Mayor Ron Animashaun. Her program areas included constituent relations and youth development.

She received her undergraduate degree in Political Science and Master's in Public Administration from Southern University and A&M College in Baton Rouge, Louisiana. Janea was initiated into the Beta Psi Chapter of Alpha Kappa Alpha Sorority, Inc., and is currently an active Omicron Lambda Omega Chapter member. She is also a 2x's best-selling lead author and featured writer in the first and second editions of the HBCU Experience Anthology: The Southern University System Edition.

In her spare time, she volunteers for local nonprofits and serves as a Daughters Beyond Incarceration and Junior Achievement Young Professionals board member. She is a founding member of the Women of Color Nonprofit Leaders for Change, a network of BIPOC (Black, Indigenous, People of Color) women leaders in philanthropy.

She is a 2023 Transatlantic Inclusion Leaders Network (TILN) Fellow. In 2022, she was recognized by the Baton Rouge Black Chamber of Commerce as a Woman of Influence. She is a 2022 Congressional Black Caucus Advocacy and Campaign Training Alumni, a 2021 Southern University Alumni Federation 40 under 40 recipient, a 2020 Institute of Politics: Loyola University New Orleans Cohort member, and a 2019 BOLD (Black Organizing for Leadership & Dignity) Fellow.

Through a commitment to service to a cause greater than self, she hopes to inspire millennials to take an active stand in their communities.

CHRISTOPHER M. LEVY

Live Gold Defend Blue
Christopher M. Levy

Hailing from the historic city of Donaldsonville, Louisiana, my connections to Southern University run deep. Donaldsonville natives include the first dean of the institution, John S. Jones, namesake to the storied freshmen men's dormitory, J. S. Jones Hall (aka Old Jones, demolished 2020) and father to Ralph Emerson Jones, second President of Grambling State University, and Governor Francis T. Nichols, who signed Act 87 into law, establishing Southern University in 1880. I discovered these little-known facts (post undergrad) through my quiet time and casual reading of Southern University history, coupled with my interest in general history. Donaldsonville has many Southern University graduates. Attending Southern is a family tradition. I am one of many family members who have matriculated or are currently experiencing Scott's Bluff. My first introduction to Southern University was one summer traveling with my Tee Linda (SU Education '75) to drop off my cousin, Lindsay (SU Engineering '05), who would be attending an SU summer enrichment program. I candidly remember crossing the hump and gasping as we passed Lacumba II, Southern's live jaguar. Little did I know that this summer trip would be the spark of my love affair with Southern University and A&M College.

As a first-year student entering Southern in the fall of 2003, I was a grounded, yet lost eighteen-year-old. I was wondering and wandering in this new world of college life. Luckily, I had a few cousins on campus to help ensure I assimilated well. They spoiled me with trips to Walmart – trust me, that was a privilege. Jones Hall was a rite of passage for men entering Southern University. This was my first time living out of my family home, and I cherished every moment. Jones Hall opened my eyes to a world outside of the normal, small-town life to which I was accustomed. The Res Life Circle during freshmen week was Intro to Networking 101. This evening activity of hanging out in "The Circle" and meeting new people was the beginning of my HBCU (Historically Black Colleges and Universities) cultural experience. The Circle was a place where lifelong friends met. There was never a dull moment. Fall of 2003 was an overload of excellence, pride, and tradition. Southern won the SWAC Football Championship, Pete Richardson's last win as head coach. *College Hill* was in production, and the campus atmosphere was vibrant. Southern had lived up to the hype! On the bluff, I found pride. Pride that runs deep as the "river that flows onto the sea." Freshman semester truly confirmed that I had made the right choice in continuing the tradition of attending Southern University. Therefore, the journey began!

Coursework under my belt, I entered the College of Business (COB), majoring in marketing. The COB played a pivotal role in molding me into the service-driven leader I am today. It took a semester or so for me to engage with COB student organizations as a reserve student. Professor Katrice Albert encouraged others and me to sharpen our skills by way of the COB Marketing & Sales Club (COBMSC), COB Student Leadership Council (COBSLC), and other COB organizations. Before long, those words of encouragement resulted in me serving as Marketing & Sales Club Public Relations Manager, COBSLC Homecoming Committee Co-Chair, and Black Executive Exchange Program (BEEP) Vice President. These leadership roles presented opportunities to create the first marketing and sales conference; personally invite business executives to visit and become mentors; organize the BEEP Career Awareness and Planning Seminar; and lend my creativity to the homecoming committee – conceptualizing Mr. and Miss College of Business. Through student organizations, I met three lifelong friends with whom I will forever share a bond: Antoria, Kim, and Anthony. We dubbed ourselves the COB Fab 4. Representing and serving the College of Business and its students was a pleasure. My passion to serve and preserve Southern University was cultivated in the halls of T.T. Allain.

While my calendar was full of COB classes and activities, I also worked full time at Albertsons. Albertsons was my first job in high school; I was the Assistant Front End Manager. If it were not for my HBCU, and its village of support that continued to pour life into me through my challenges, or Ms. Albert's continuously demanding excellence, I would not be the driven, well-rounded professional I am today. Balancing school, work, and life was a struggle; however, it was necessary in my development as a leader and an advocate of HBCU students.

On December 12, 2008, I became an alumnus of Southern University and A&M College. However, my work to preserve its legacy was just beginning. By March of 2009, I decided to move and settled in Dallas, Texas. Dallas, unbeknownst to me, was home to hundreds of Jaguars and a highly active alumni chapter. Joining the Dallas alumni chapter afforded me the chance to rub shoulders with Southernites who were movers and shakers in the DFW Metroplex. I appreciated the longevity and excellence of Southern, and further honed my leadership skills. As I volunteered and learned the functions of the alumni chapter, I was charged with helping the chapter engage and invite young alumni. Chapter President LaQuitta Thomas appointed me co-chair of the newly formed Y2K Jags committee with the charge in mind. Our committee created the chapter's first day party series, Dallas Jags Connect, in an effort to provide a space for DFW area Southernites, young and seasoned, to chat, connect, and celebrate being a Jaguar. While a member of the Dallas chapter, I served on the student relations committee, Bayou Bash committee (chapter annual crawfish boil fundraiser 35+ years), Founders Golf Tournament committee, and second vice president/membership committee chair. Serving as an alumni recruiter helped me connect my passion, Southern University, and my purpose, student advocacy. Conversing with young adults regarding career goals, and the Southern University experience, became second nature. This is a testament to the knowledge of Southern University, and college and career readiness.

After living in Dallas for ten years, I returned to Louisiana and Southern University with passion and purpose in tow. Today, as an employee of the university, I am influencing and transforming lives daily. Serving as the university scholarship counselor, my goal is to assist students with maximizing all resources and engaging as many alumni mentors as possible. Currently, I continue to preserve the legacy of Southern through the Southern University Alumni Federation (SUAF). I was appointed Southern University Young Alumni Network (SUYAN) – National Chair. SUYAN works to engage and recognize the achievements of young alumni, while increasing the membership and programs of SUAF. My HBCU story continues as I was elected as the Southern University Alumni Federation Historian for the 2022-2024 term. Servicing Southern and the Jaguar Nation started as a passion, but I am convinced it is my purpose.

Our alma mater states, "We owe our all to thee!" I most certainly do.

About Christopher M. Levy

Christopher M. Levy is a native of Donaldsonville, La. He is a fall 2008 graduate of the College of Business at Southern University with a B.S. in Marketing - Professional Sales.

Christopher resides in Denham Springs, LA and currently serves as the Scholarship Coordinator at Southern University and A&M College. Through his role, Christopher educates minority, first generation, & undeserved students on the financial aid process and resources available for college, motivates students through their matriculation, and advocates on students behave. Christopher prides himself on ensuring the best student experience.

Christopher is a life member of the Southern University Alumni Federation (SUAF). He is in his first term as the SUAF Historian (2022-2024) As Historian, Christopher's collaborates with fellow executive board members to curate events and campaigns that yield increase alumni engagement and membership. Christopher is the immediate past Southern University Young Alumni Network (SUYAN) National Chair. As National Chair, he led a team of young alumni in developing engagement programs geared toward increasing membership of SUAF. Under his leadership, SUYAN worked to cultivate a culture of philanthropy, reached 1500 paid alumni members under the age of 40, expanded its footprint to ten SUAF chapter cities, and now manages the SUAF 40 Under Forty awards.

Christopher spends his spare time cooking, traveling, and recruiting for Southern University.

AYANNA C. SPIVEY

The H stands for Historically…
Ayanna C. Spivey

HBCUs are not a trend. HBCUs have been foundational in the success and upper mobility of Black Americans. HBCUs were founded to provide education to free slaves and their descendants. The Higher Education Act of 1965 deemed historically Black colleges or universities that were established prior to 1964 where the primary "mission was, and is, the education of black Americans, and that is accredited by a nationally recognized accrediting agency or association determined by the Secretary [of Education] to be a reliable authority as to the quality of training offered or is, according to such an agency or association, making reasonable progress toward accreditation." These institutions have over a hundred years of molding our nation's Black leaders and professionals. Southern University was founded in 1880, after three delegates from the Louisiana State Constructional Convention presented the idea to fund an institution of higher education for people of color. In 1914, Southern University relocated to Baton Rouge, after being designated a land-grant college to be closer to more rural Louisiana residents along with racial motivated pressures. Southern University is now the largest HBCU in Louisiana and the only HBCU system in the country.

The Spivey college journey started when my grandmother, Bennie Ruth Spivey, entered Southern University in the fall of 1954 pursuing a degree in accounting. She was an athlete and member of the newly established women's basketball team. Graduating in three years, she returned to Bogalusa working in the public sector and later became self-employed as a tax-preparer. When my father, her youngest son, George P. Spivey III, returned home from being stationed overseas and with her new daughter-in-law from California, Lisa R. Remson. My grandmother greeted them with a warm welcome of job applications and completed applications to Southern University. After getting acclimated to a new state and married life, George and Lisa moved to Baton Rouge from Bogalusa, to start their journey as Jaguars in the fall of 1986. My parents were also expecting their first child while living in married-student housing. Throughout that unique experience of being married and raising a child, in Fall 1991 my mother was the first to graduate receiving a Bachelor's of Science in Therapeutic Recreation crossing the stage expecting their second child, me! In 1996, both my brother and I were able to watch them graduate with their degrees, our father receiving a Bachelor of Science in Institutional Management and our mother receiving her Master of Science in Therapeutic Recreation. Through varied life circumstances, the Spivey family moved to Roswell, GA and finally settled back in my mother's home state of Southern California. Our parents later divorced in 1999, but that Southern legacy stayed ingrained.

Being born in the shadow of Southern University, attending major events and watching the Human Jukebox practices, the love and fascination never changed for my brother and I. In person experiences transitioned to watching Southern on television. Tuned into the Bayou Classic every year in our living room and every Wednesday, in 2004m watching BET's College Hill, Southern became the most famous HBCU to me. I know that was where I was going. From the beginning it wasn't a question, my brother and I aspired to be the drum major and I the Dancing Dolls captain. When the time came for me to apply to college, of course Southern was the first application I completed, my mother decided it was time to take me to the Bayou Classic. That was the rubber stamp needed to get into Southern by any means necessary. Two days after my 18th birthday that following, I was on a plan to Baton Rouge starting my Southern adventure.

As a third-generation Jaguar felt like a dream and I hit the ground running. Starting with student government association as a freshman class senator, then becoming Miss Sophomore 2011-2012. Followed by, a Fall 2011 initiate of the Alpha Tau Chapter of Delta Sigma Theta Sorority, Inc., as well as becoming the Association for Women's Students Chief of Staff and a student coordinator for new student orientation. The lasting accomplishment has been serving as the 83rd Miss Southern University and A&M College. That experience alone allowed me to represent my college across the country, be amongst the first student leaders to return to the NASAP Student Leadership Institution (SLI), became a trophy girl for the Mc Donald's 365 Black Awards, be featured in two commercials for the university, and became the first Miss Souther to be a part of the Top 10 Ebony HBCU Campus Queens. Though my HBCU undergraduate matriculation ended after receiving my Bachelor of Interdisciplinary Studies with a concentration in Social Work and Sociology, my HBCU journey has developed into a lifelong one.

These experiences led me to work in higher education, specifically in the California community college system. I have worked in equity-based programs covering various underserved and incarcerated student populations. I have been an advocate for the California Community College HBCU Transfer agreement in promoting HBCU attendance of community college students. I also created a nonprofit to promote higher learning at HBCUs and inspire academic excellence through college preparation. I am still a part of the Southern Sisters, an organization of former and current Southern University class and campus queens. While pursuing my Master of Science in Higher Education Leadership and Student Development, I consistently presented work on HBCUs and the Black student experience. I am now embarking on my Ph.D. journey with HBCUs and the education of Black people as the primary focus.

Southern University is intertwined within my familial lineage and experience, it is an extreme privilege to share this honor of being an alumna of the Southern University and A&M College with my mother, father, and grandmother. It has been a life-changing experience for all of us. I am also proud to say that HBCUs have a deep history within my extended family who represent HBCUs such as Howard University, Oakwood University, Langston University, Clark Atlanta University, and Tuskegee University. These HBCUs of the like, and more specifically Southern University, have produced quality doctors, lawyers, nurses, therapists, educators, entrepreneurs, philanthropists, politicians, judges, influencers, and creatives. Again, HBCUs are not a trend but they are a legacy that you can create and/or follow to chart your own path to make a global impact. Let these stories to follow be just a snippet of how an HBCU education can enhance your life path. Geaux Jags!

About Ayanna C. Spivey

Ayanna Spivey was born in the shadow of Southern University in Baton Rouge, LA. She was raised in Moreno Valley, Ca. Ayanna's leadership skills and creativity revealed themselves early in her childhood from being involved in her home church's youth ministry, youth choir, youth council, and various social events. She really explored those skills while in high school lettering in 3 sports, active in Associated Student Body, Black Student Union, and the becoming the Southern California Regional President of Black Student Unions. These experiences laid the foundation for her time at Southern University and the beginning of her career in higher education, through various positions in the Student Government Association, Miss Sophomore and then Miss Southern on the Royal Court. She also took part in the new student summer orientations, football recruiting, and being a member of the Alpha Tau chapter of Delta Sigma Theta Sorority Inc. All these endeavors sparked the ideas of wanting to go into higher education. Upon graduating from Southern University with a Bachelors in Interdisciplinary Studies, with a concentration in Social Work and Sociology, she returned to California and received a Masters of Science in Higher Education leadership and Student Development from California Baptist University.

With the completion of her secondary and post-secondary education, in 2016 she launched We Are Educated, LLC. We Are Educated, LLC is an organization that strives to promote higher learning at HBCUs and inspire academic excellence through college preparation. It is the organization's belief that it can play a part in the increase of HBCU attendance by highlighting the benefits of the overall HBCU experience. We Are Educated, LLC provides scholarships to assist undergraduate students with their matriculation through various workshops and fairs. We Are Educated, LLC has provided about $3000 plus in giving within its first two years. In 2021, We Are Educated, LLC transitioned to We Are Educated, Incorporated and is a tax-exempt 501c3 company continuing the efforts of its origin in 2016.

Since her career path continued in California, Ayanna has worked within the California Community College system going on 7 years working with various programs that includes academic counseling, student services, academic success programs and within the California Department of Corrections and Rehabilitation. Her passions for equity and student success are evident in the work that she does within her perspective departments by always putting the students and their interests first. It is her hope to continue within the community college system will start her journey in pursuing her PhD in Cultural Studies at Claremont Graduate University in the fall of 2022. In the meantime, she continues to be active with the Southern University Alumni Federation Alumni Los Angeles Chapter, Southern University Young Alumni Network. She was named as one of SU's 40 Under Forty for the inaugural cohort in 2018.

DELANO HOLMES

Ol' Yard Boy
Delano Holmes

As far back as I can remember, I've always been intrigued by the Black College Experience. Having grown up in Los Angeles, California, shows like *A Different World* and movies like *School Daze* further sparked my interest in HBCUs. I was afforded the opportunity to attend The Southern University and A&M college in Baton Rouge, Louisiana, in the fall of 2000. Being from LA, The HBCU scene was somewhat of a culture shock. There were beautiful shades of brown everywhere. The different accents, dialects, styles of clothing, and all around swag was mind blowing. With most of my family being from South of Louisiana, I was aware of both Southern University and Grambling State University. However, being aware and actually walking the yard were two totally different situations. It was always a dream of mine to be on television, so I decided, initially, to major in theater. After a little research, I chose journalism as my focus of study. With football being my secondary focus, I dreamed of playing in The Bayou Classic, which I had watched on television since I was a little kid. I have four older cousins that went to Grambling University, and they all played football. They would always brag about the Bayou Classic experience; again, this was something that I really looked forward to. I had no idea what I was getting myself into. I was in no way prepared for what the experience would be.

My first week alone was wild. Freshman move-in was an eye opening experience. My mother and I arrived on campus, and I immediately noticed a Sea of Black faces. There were different shades of brown, and all the different accents were intriguing. I was assigned a dorm room: Jones Hall, 5th floor, room 506 D, to be exact. As we pulled up to the dorm, I thought to myself, hmm… this looks like the *Good Times* projects. I started to move my stuff into the dorm and really wanted to get settled in. Before leaving, my mom looked at me and said, "you are here now, and you have something to do. Make sure you leave here with everything you came with and everything you came to get." At that point, it was all on me.

My first semester at Southern was cool. I finished the semester on the Dean's list and looked forward to the spring semester. Unbeknownst to me, that fall semester was filled with occurrences, one, of which, I, in no way, prepared for, nor could even imagine happening. My mother, Constance Marie Holmes, passed away. This could not have come at a worse time. I was a freshman in college, yet, all of a sudden, I was faced with the task of raising a nine-year-old little brother. The world as I knew it had drastically changed. For the first time in life, I doubted myself. I figured that I would not be able to continue college and achieve the goals that I set forth prior to attending Southern University. I questioned myself. Could I do it? How would I make it by myself? Could I afford this? Would I ever be on TV? Would I ever be successful? How do I enjoy this experience and be a positive role model to my little brother? There are a lot of things in this world that I am grateful for. One of them is Pearle Mae Brown. My grandmother and Ace boon coon. Pearlie Mae stepped right on up and told me that she had my back 100%. I had a goal to accomplish, and she would do her best to make sure I kept my promise to my mother, so we kept striving.

I met a lot of interesting people during my time on the yard. I developed a lot of friendships that I hold dear to my heart today. My main crew of friends were mostly from New Orleans, My Guy, Eddie Green, and Kendrick Paul were my main running mates, and we got into a whole lot of calamities. Half the people I knew on campus thought I was from New Orleans and were surprised to find out that I was actually from Los Angeles.

In some cases, we, as students, meet individuals that have lifelong impacts on our lives. In my case, I was blessed to have influential instructors that made an impact on my life. Jeff Thomas Sr. was a teacher in the Math department. He had an extremely humorous and crafty teaching style. He captivated students by giving riddles and life lessons that would actually make you think. He would ask things like, "How far can you run into the woods? Students would look at each other like, *huh?*, and, to be honest, I dropped that class. I hated Math. Although I did drop that class, I would always visit his office to talk about whatever was on my mind. He never faulted me for dropping the class, and he always accepted me with open arms. Rother Thomas became one of my mentors as I began to seek out Omega Psi Phi. He is one of my closest friends. There was one more Professor at Southern that really stuck out: Dr. Troy Allen, who taught African American Studies, and this brother was deep. He was a smooth player from Pittsburgh. His main goal was to show the importance of being a strong man/woman. He was dedicated to his students and took a liking to me. I would chat it up with him daily After graduation, I would often pop up on him and it was the same love. Dr. Allen passed away in March of 2017, and the yard hasn't been the same since. The effect that both of these men had on my life will last forever. Rest In Peace, Dr. Troy Allen.

By this time, I was in the full swing of things, and, honestly, I dropped the ball with the whole football thing–no pun intended. However, man, was I grooving! Baton had a lot to offer at the time, and I had my hand in all of it... I started seriously rapping and took a shot at acting. I was always the class clown type, so it came naturally to me. I formed a group, we called ourselves the Imitators. I was a master beat boxer and could sing pretty well, so the group would imitate different artists and songs while bringing a comedic element to each performance. My brother Y.Luck (Keith Swanier) and Justin "DJ JUICE" Patterson formed the group. We entered five talent shows. We won all five and never looked back. By this time, my name was buzzing around campus, and, like *School Daze*, the brothers of Omega Psi Phi caught my eye. Around this same time, there was talk around the yard about a reality show audition. Now, over the years, we heard talks of shows and movies coming to campus, so, initially, we thought it was just another fly-by chance situation. However, to everyone's surprise, BET was on campus and in full effect. There were long lines in the student union as students filled out applications. Now, these applications were at least twenty pages long. With that being said, I grabbed one, filled out the first page and wrote phrases I dare not repeat throughout the rest of the package. Meanwhile, BET was also doing a little leg work, moving around campus asking who were some of the more popular students on campus. My name came up numerous times. I looked at myself as the heavy-set Dwayne Wayne with way more Swag. But seriously, I was initially selected to interview for the show. During the interview, I met Tracey Edmonds. I made up a story telling Tracy that I was single-handedly responsible for Baby Face's success, and I was the person who gave him the name, Baby Face. Tracey replied as if she was astonished. Others in the room laughed as Tracey realized that I wasn't even born when Face got started. I was instantly in. From there, we shot a pilot with myself and seven other students. The pilot was a hit; however, they needed to replace a few of the cast members. Eventually the cast was set and it was time for filming. We all moved into the dorms on campus, and it was crazy all over. We filmed, for the most part, during the fall 2003 semester. At the same time that semester, I was participating in membership selection with the brothers of Omega Psi Phi. Our initiation Probate premiered on the last episode of the season

The cast was full of characters. We had the wild child, Kinda. We had the frat boy, Gabrielle. We had the Jock, K-mack. Lastly, we had the Southern Belle, Veronica, among others. And then there was ME… Lano, the entertainment extraordinaire. NO CAP. Gabriel was my roommate, Gabe, in the band, and he was a member of Alpha Phi Alpha fraternity, so we were able to get along pretty well. Surprisingly, we all got along really well as a cast. Relationships were developed that lasted to this day. I wasn't the oldest in the cast, but I had an old soul, so, lots of times, I shared wisdom with my fellow castmates that helped them get through what it was that was bothering them. I guess you can say I was the big brother. I ran around terrorizing the campus as Kevin excelled on the football field. Jabari faced a few difficult situations during our time filming, and I tried my best to give as much help as possible.

Filming, social life, and our Scholastic responsibilities made it difficult at times; however, I wouldn't trade the experience for the world. *College Hill* premiered in the spring of 2003. It was an instant success. Millions of black teens were afforded the opportunity to see, first-hand, what it was like to attend an HBCU. We were instantly famous. My little brother would go to school every day and brag about how his big brother was a TV star. And my Granny! Good Lord, my grandmother would brag and tell all her friends at church, and in the community, that her baby was on TV. She would Say "girl, my grandbaby on the BET." I was extremely proud of the fact that we were actually able to go to my grandmother's house and film a couple of episodes so Pearlie was able to get her shine on. That meant a lot to me, and for that I am forever grateful.

Being on the first season of *College Hill* was a blessing. It was the first of its kind. An All Black College reality series. I thank Tracey Edmonds and BET for the opportunity to launch my career. After College Hill, I went on to star in multiple films and sitcoms. I received my degree in the fall of 2005; I was able to keep my promise that I made it to my mother four years prior. I was also able to stand as a true testament of what hard work and dedication can do. I'm grateful to my mother and My Auntee Nita for keeping US out of those California streets, as much as they could Lol.

No matter what you're faced with, if you put your faith in God and stay determined, there are no limits to what you can accomplish. I continue to act, write, and produce film and television shows in Los Angeles, California. I also currently have two businesses in the Los Angeles area. A Cosmetic line SASSY SUGA, and a New Orleans style food eatery that specializes in New Orleans style SnowBalls called SNEAUX BIDNESS. I am a brand ambassador and creative lead for DOPEAHOLIC, a nationwide cannabis company that focuses on bringing awareness to the culture, lifestyle, and brand. With the success of *College Hill*, I was able to open many doors for myself as well as inspire thousands of kids nationwide to attend HBCUs. Most importantly, my little brother. As an adult, I choose human services as an addition to my entertainment work. I invest in people and help people overcome setbacks through a homeless service company, Volunteers of America. That love, understanding, and care are all characteristics of that old Southern spirit, which I learned at My HBCU. I am blessed and overly grateful...... O Southern, Dear Southern…

About Delano Holmes

Delano Mitchell Holmes is an actor, comedian, writer and entrepreneur from Los Angeles. He has enjoyed success in television and film for close to eighteen years. Once considered the "Black Belushi" by theatre Professor M. Rutland (Southern University School of Arts), Holmes has been able to deliver knee-slapping humor to audiences for years. Most recently, he can be seen aside Slink Johnson playing Detective Mitchell in the movie *Dirty Cops LA* (2021). He has also entertained audiences as "Avery" in the movie *A Gift Horse* and as "Spook" in *Da Block Party*.

Delano was raised in South Central, Los Angeles by his mother, Constance Marie Holmes. As a youth, he was faced with the daily trials of an African American man growing up in the inner cities of Los Angeles. As a product of a single-parent home, Delano was determined to succeed in both academics and athletics as a student at Westchester High School. It was his goal to not only excel in the classroom and on the football field, but to stand as a positive role model to his younger brother, Mark Lawson. Delano graduated high school with honors and chose "The" Southern University A&M College to further his collegiate academics. Delano received his B.A. in Journalism from Southern University and A&M College in 2005, as he had promised his mother he would after her untimely death in January of 2001.

While at Southern, Delano was an active member of The Southern University Student Government Association, Men's Federation and Southern University football team. In the fall of 2003, Delano was initiated into the Beta Sigma Chapter of Omega Psi Phi Fraternity, Inc. In that same year, Delano made his acting debut on BET's *College Hill*, which was the first all African American reality TV series. Later that year, he co-starred as "Spook" in the 2004 movie, *Da Block Party*. Since then, Delano has appeared in over sixteen films and two television series. During his eighteen-year acting career, he has worked with Chevy Chase, Mike Epps, Richard Dreyfus, Sherman Helmsley, Lou Diamond-Phillips, Clifton Powell, Carl Anthony Paine, Darrin Henson, Persia White, Joe Torry, Tracey Edmonds, Meagan Good, Ruby Dee, and John Snyder.

After graduation, Delano taught grade school English and Theatre in schools in New Orleans. As an entrepreneur, Delano focused on bringing the southern customs and traditions to Los Angeles. In 2020, Delano opened the first Sneaux Bidness, LLC, which is a New Orleans style eatery that specializes in New Orleans style Snowballs and cuisine. Delano is also co-owner of Sassy Suga Lips service, which is a beauty and health cosmetics brand located in L.A. Delano stands as a brand ambassador and creative lead of Dopeaholics, an L.A.-based lifestyle brand company that promotes culture and cannabis that believes in Making America Dope Again.

Delano currently works as a Program Manager for Volunteers of America in the greater Los Angeles area. He also overseas a National Youth Build program. That Youth Build program focusses on providing young adults aged 17-24 the opportunity to attain their high school diploma through John Muir Charter School. The program also offers a construction and/or automotive trade through The Maxine Waters Employment Preparation Center located in Watts, California.

Delano has maintained a positive image in his community and professional career. He has homed in on his own craft and creating a style of comedy that moves fluidly from scene to scene. Delano credits his grandmother, Ms. Pearl Mae Brown, for his hard work ethic, witty punchlines, and all-around crafty humor. Although he is able to portray a wide variety of dialects and personalities, many of the performances in his films are to pay homage to friends and family members of rural southern Louisiana. His family ties to the south allow him to capture those heartfelt, humorous, soulful characteristics of "down home" and bring those characters to life. As a man, his biggest task is to continue to stand as that positive role model for his brother and others in his family and community.

GABRIEL D. LANGLEY "JY"

The Start of Something Great
Gabriel D. Langley "JY"

My college experience was what I hoped it would be, but it was also quite different from what I thought it would be. Attending Southern University, my first introduction was crab week in the band. And although I heard the stories and the rumors, it was still more mentally demanding than I could have imagined. The expectations from my fellow band members and freshman crab brothers were unwavering. No one gave you a pass. No one accepted your excuses either. You were either good enough, or you weren't. Although my personality was always to be the best, it was a jaw-dropping reality that now I was in a room full of talented individuals, and my best was no longer good enough. The challenge was on.

The first semester of my academic year is mostly a blur because of how much time I spent adjusting to band life of this caliber. However, the friends and relationships that we built in that band room were forged forever. Dr. Isaac Gregg was a pure inspiration because he always expected everything from you. His motto that molded my personality for the next four years and beyond was, "Be at the right place at the right time with the right equipment, ready to concentrate." I attended Southern University on a music scholarship, and my degree course was Biology and Music Performance. I found mentors and inspiration in many different professors over the years. Musically, the other associate band director, Mr. Lawrence Jackson, taught me that your energy is contagious. If you're having fun, so will those you are there to entertain. Associate Director Mr. Cornell Knighten told us, "Demand your worth, but never sacrifice your integrity." Mr. Alvin Baptiste taught me the passion behind New Orleans jazz and improvisation. Academically, I was pushed to be better by Dr. Willis Jacob and Dr. Fitzgerald Spencer of the Biology

Department, which helped me achieve multiple Honor Society inductions and to receive an invitation to the 2005 Endocrinology Symposium in San Diego, California. This also led to me being one of the representatives for Southern University at the BKX and NIS Conference in Richmond, Virginia in 2005 and being invited to the Endocrinology Symposium in San Diego, California in 2005. Lastly, my worldview and social ideology were turned upside down when I took a mandatory cultural class: the African American Experience (Psychology) with Dr. Reginald Rackley.

Everything you thought you knew about your Blackness was challenged as his curriculum exposed you to the unknown influences of today's society. For me, it has been one of the more significant factors contributing to navigating my life, utilizing my social circles, and gauging my success. Having professors see your potential, and their willingness to be a resource to you, meant everything to me. They gave me structure and forced me to elevate my character to the person they saw in me. Yes, I partied with the best of them. Yes, I lived the Greek life and won step shows with Alpha Phi Alpha and Kappa Kappa Psi Band Fraternity. However, when I reflect on my college experience, I realize how demanding my professors were of my success and how invested they were in me to rise to the challenge. This, to me, was the HBCU Experience.

In the early fall of 2003, there was a buzz around campus about a pilot reality TV show being filmed. Little was known or seen, but everyone knew it was happening. Then, as the official school year kicked off, it became evident that BET had a reality TV show planned for students on campus. They were holding auditions to fill the cast. I had no interest in being a part of any reality show. But one day, the casting crew showed up in the band room. Later, I learned that they were looking for a cast member to highlight Greek life on campus. And, in grand fashion, Dr. Greggs said, "KK Psi and band is the biggest fraternity on campus. If you want to capture the Greek experience, then you need to follow the Southern University Band."

Of course, we all cheered in agreement until we realized we all had to undergo the long interview process. Again, not having much desire to be on the show, I went through the motions and answered their questions. Then, the band went outside to perform a show for them to get visuals on everyone they were interested in. After that, the idea was no more than an afterthought. About a week later, I received a phone call asking if I was interested in the show. By this time, my tuition situation had changed. I lost part of my scholarship due to a clerical error and could not pay for housing. I was currently sleeping on the hard floor of my frat brother's dorm room. They wanted me to join the cast since I was in the band, plus KK Psi, Alpha Phi Alpha, and somewhat entertaining. I just needed that room and board to get off that cold floor. So, I packed my things and moved into the dorm room set on campus.

Our season was heavily based on following eight students as they experienced everyday college life at an HBCU. The camera crews followed us to class. They followed us to events on campus and off campus, and they filmed us interacting with each other as cast members (good, bad, and ugly). We created many memories and moments. But there are a few that stand out the most to me. The first one was our fan boat tour of the Louisiana bayou. This was an experience like no other, jumping on a fan boat and cruising through the narrow creeks of the Louisiana swamp land and witnessing all of the crazy interesting lifestyles that go along with it. It was a family-owned and operated business that took us on the Bayou Tour. To this day, we all talk about the patriarch of the family, whom they enduringly called Cappy (Captain-Pappy). He was an older man with a spry step. He spoke with a heavy accent in what seemed to be a mix between Southern twain and French that seemingly only his son could understand. Everyone laughed when he laughed—not because we knew what he said funny—but because we couldn't understand him, and he laughed so hard, showing off his one or two teeth in front. No greater memory of that day stands out than when Cappy was showing us how to feed the flathead catfish of the bayou with dog food. Delano leaned over the edge of the boat to get a better look at the fish, and his cell phone stored in his top shirt pocket took a swim in the dark and muddy water. Yes, it was gone for good, and yes, Cappy laughed, so we laughed, except for Delano.

Another great memory was when we, as a cast, got in trouble for not obeying the rules for keeping the production team up to date on our whereabouts and agendas. It wasn't intentional. But for most of us, we were juniors and seniors. So, we were always on the go. Having to tell someone where we were going, what we were doing, and who we were going to be with seems like a return to parental supervision. So, the production team decided to get their point across by having the drill sergeant for the Marine ROTC give us his version of punishment with 5 a.m. PT and team building. As you would expect, he and his team came in, yelling and waking everyone up. They were no joke. It quickly became physical with the push-ups, sit-ups, running, and carrying the team tree log. Everyone still had crust in their eyes, and the ladies had their hair tied up from sleep. However, I was fresh off a night of partying and had just walked through the door at 4 a.m. So, it was all jokes to me. They didn't like me laughing at the camera.

We had fun on top of fun and made memories that we laugh about to this day. But during that time, we had no idea of the impact and history we were making for HBCU campuses nationwide. We didn't realize we were the first all-Black cast reality TV show until commercials started rolling out. I literally had news reporters sitting in my living room during the first episode watch party. That premiere season of *College Hill* on BET quickly became the number one show on the network. After hundreds of interviews and news articles about this "all-Black cast" reality show, we noticed the positive impact of youth interest in HBCUs.

Edmond entertainment and BET found a creative way to dismiss the stigmas of attending a historically Black college and university by highlighting the everyday life of eight college students being positive, attending classes, parties, events, being sociable, and being involved on campus. They showed students enjoying Greek life, cheer life, athletic life, and being popular—or not so popular. Most importantly, they show that it is okay to be all those things or none of those things as you journey through college to find yourself. The enrollment at SU increased beyond expectations that fall semester, and the internet's outcry for another season was proof that we had started something great.

About Gabriel D. Langley "JY"

Gabriel D. Langley is a creative and spirited personality from Dallas, Texas who uses his gift in the business and entertainment worlds. He attended Southern University and A& M College in Baton Rouge, Louisiana, where he initially studied Biology and Music Performance.

With entertainment being a big part of his life, in 2004, he began pursuing a career in entertainment professionally. Gabriel got his start as a model with notable work, posing for Dobbs & Krave Magazine, Runway shows for Coogi, photoshoots for Ed Hardie, and working with great stylists such as Rick Davy (NY) and Tracy Kennedy (LA). Under the alias Gabriel D. Angell, he's performed on trumpet with Tito "TJ" Jackson, Jr., Rickey Smiley, Erykah Badu, Tichina Arnold, and Groove University Live Band. Gabriel has performed on drums with Mark Hildreth, J-Pop Artist Takao, NY77 L.A. Funk Band, and others. As an actor, Gabriel has starred and featured in many films, including *Spades-4 Of A Kind*, *Black Angels*, *Searching -The Movie*, *He Heard My Cry*, *Mouthpiece*, *Sex & Violence*, and *Walter*. He also has made television appearances on shows such as *Blood Relatives*, *Friday Night Lights*, the Original Season of BET's *College Hill* at Southern University, and the hit German Detective TV Series *Carsten Stahl-PrivatDetektiv*.

Gabriel is also a serial entrepreneur, starting with his sports fitness and in-home personal training service in 2005 and musician management in 2006. As a foundation for his entrepreneurial spirit, he worked to develop a trade-in credit development and finance. This trade opened the door to contract and consulting work. Gabriel quickly diversified his non-traditional financial education by working with companies such as Debt Relief America and Westlake Financial Services, and consulting with New Sky Funding and Out of Box Business Funding & Development. Gabriel then advanced to his current role as partner at AG Management & Business Consulting, working with small businesses on strategic management and business relationships.

After years of investing and working with startups, Gabriel looked for a franchise opportunity and fell in love with being an authorized dealer for FUBU Mobile. Yes! The clothing brand. A couple of years later, Gabriel and his business team were granted control of the Master Agency and Business Operations. Now that FUBU is "in the business of connecting people," he and his teams' current goal is to elevate FUBU Mobile by growing the brand's trust in the telecommunication industry, promoting economic growth and championing social unity in the community. For Us, By Us/For Unity, By Unity. As Gabriel continues to manage and consult with businesses, he decided to return to school and pursue a post-graduate education in Business Psychology.

Gabriel ultimately wants to be an asset to the communities that have helped groom him over the years. He wants to continue to grow his involvement in uplifting those in need with his nonprofit company, Village Inspiration Project (V.I.P.). Gabriel looks forward to building on the work he's done and using his connections and resources to break down barriers holding aspiring youth from achieving success.

WAYNE J. HAYDIN JR., J.D.

Mr. President
Wayne J. Haydin Jr., J.D.

When people hear about my HBCU experience, inevitably the first thing they always ask is "how did THAT happen? How did you end up THERE?" Then they ask, "what was THAT like?"

It was the greatest time of my life. So much so that on the day of my graduation in 2004, I had still not packed my dorm room because I didn't want to leave the place that had become my home. Why would I want to leave? For a white guy like me growing up in racist Louisiana where I didn't align with racism, Southern was my "safe space." People on the outside looking in would often wonder how I was treated, but my time at S.U. was when I was the most at peace.

I was born in and raised in the New Orleans East area of the 9th Ward. I attended Orleans Parish Public Schools from Kindergarten all the way through High School. My Kindergarten teacher was a Southern Alum. My 6th Grade teacher was a Southern Alum. When I got to Middle School, my band director was a Southern Alum, and I was the only white kid in the band. By the time I got to Abramson High School, not only was I the only white kid in the band, but I was the only white kid in all of the public-school bands in all of New Orleans. It was there at Abramson that I got the nickname "Uncle Buck" from a fellow bandsman. By my senior year, I was completely immersed in the band culture of New Orleans. Upon graduation, I had no desire to march for any college band other than Southern University.

By that time, my best friend/brother Reginald also had an influence on my college choice. He and I had been friends since the 3rd grade, and his entire family were Southern Alumni. One day after band practice during our Senior year we were walking down the street and I had a momentary lapse of judgment, saying out loud "I think I might go to Grambling." Without warning he slapped me across the back of my head, pointed at me dead in my face and sternly said "we don't do that!"

Me going to Southern was a natural progression and a perfect fit. Whereas many African American students choose to attend an HBCU because they spent their entire youth in predominantly white schools, my situation was the opposite. Many black students coming from white schools experience a bit of culture shock when they first arrive on campus, but I did not. I felt at home. Many of the other students from New Orleans already knew who I was, and as such, the "Uncle Buck" nickname followed me up to Baton Rouge.

After a few years, when there was an open position for an RA in my dorm, the other guys in the house encouraged me to apply. This was the first time I realized how much I was respected by my peers and that they felt I was a good candidate to be in a position of leadership. They didn't want an "outsider" to come into our home to be the RA. They wanted me to take the position because I was viewed as "one of them." It was around the same time that I had begun to get involved with Student Government as well. By the time my final year came around, I was encouraged by my peers to seek the Presidency, as I was considered the best candidate and logical "next man up" for the job. After a grassroots campaign with a skeleton crew on a shoestring budget, we won by a landslide. It was a great time and a great feeling on the Yard. People still speak of it with fond memories all these years later, and while I find it flattering to this day, I still maintain that my election isn't a story about ME. It's a story about SOUTHERN, and how my classmates at Southern knew how much grief they would get from the rest of the HBCU community for electing a white President but didn't care. The overwhelming sentiment was that although I was white, I was a jaguar who bled blue and gold, and just like my housemates who had encouraged me to be an RA a few years earlier, they felt as though I was "one of them." That's why it's outrageous when people ask me how I was treated at Southern. I show them a picture on my phone of me escorting my Miss Southern, Kyana Stewart, with her crown and scepter and tell them "I was treated like royalty."

When I think back to when I was SGA President, I think about how I had the honor of literally sitting at a table and breaking bread with actual legends and giants in the history of the University; people who are no longer with us and whose names are now on some of the buildings on campus. In my opinion, at no point was this more evident than when I met the Southern 16 and had the honor of receiving my diploma during the same ceremony where they were finally awarded their degrees from Southern after being expelled in 1960 for participating in the Baton Rouge sit-ins. It was one of the most humbling experiences of my life, and the irony of them receiving their diplomas along with a white SGA President after being expelled for civil rights demonstrations has never been lost on me.

Another one of those legends who had a profound effect on my years at Southern was the late Ms. Yvonne Hughes, the former director of housing. In 1999, after a hiatus of two years from Southern, I quit my job and headed back to Baton Rouge. I had no housing application, but I still walked up to the desk and asked what I had to do to get a room as if the semester wasn't starting in two weeks. Ms. Hughes heard me and recognized me from my previous stay on the Yard when I was in the band. She pulled me into her office and told me "I'm going to put you with your buddies (bandsmen and N.O. natives) in White Hall." Horace G. White Hall became my home for the next five years of my life.

Ms. Hughes took care of me at a time when I had no family support or safety net. When I became President, she told me she wasn't just happy, but personally proud of me.

Ms. Hughes was the epitome of why I along with so many others chose to attend an HBCU; because the faculty, staff, and employees become our family who care for us and nurture us. They watch our back and catch us when we fall, taking a personal interest in making sure they provide us with everything they can to see us succeed. Ms. Hughes was one of the people who made Southern University special.

In 1999 Ms. Hughes helped me come home, welcomed me with open arms like a prodigal Son, and became my family. We are bestowed our relatives by birth, but our FAMILY are those who are chosen for us and by us through our circumstances in life, the love we give, and the love we receive.

Prior to 1999, the only place I ever considered "home" was New Orleans. Today, I tell people without hesitation that Southern University is my home, and the Jaguar Nation is my family. I will always love my home and will always love my family. That was my HBCU experience at Southern University. Aside from my education and personal growth, it was an experience of love and family that continues to this day. Southern University not only gave me my Jaguar family, but my immediate family as well. I met my wife Tareka at Southern, and we were married two weeks after I graduated from the Southern University Law Center. Today we live in the Atlanta suburb of Gwinnett County with our two sons, Wayne and David.

About Wayne J. Haydin Jr., J.D.

Wayne J. Haydin Jr., affectionately known by the Jaguar Nation as "Uncle Buck," is a native of New Orleans, LA who now resides in Gwinnett County, GA just outside of Atlanta. He is a 2004 graduate of the Nelson Mandela School of Public Policy and Urban Affairs at Southern University and A&M College in Baton Rouge, LA with a Bachelor of Arts in Political Science, as well as a former member of the Southern University Human Jukebox Marching Band. Prior to his enrollment at SUBR, he had also attended Southern University at New Orleans (SUNO). He returned to Southern in 2006 to attend the Southern University Law Center, where he was awarded his Juris Doctorate in 2009. While at SULC, he served in the Student Bar Association, was chosen as Editor In Chief of the "Public Defender," and was also inducted into the American Inns of Court as well as the A.P. Turead Chapter of Phi Alpha Delta Law Fraternity.

While in law school at Southern, Wayne worked as a Prison Interviewer with the District Court Bail Bond Program in East Baton Rouge Parish Prison, and also as an Extern Prosecutor for the East Baton Rouge District Attorney's Office under then ADA Ronald Gathe, Jr. Upon graduation he spent several years in the same Court as the Judicial Law Clerk for the Hon. Judge Trudy M. White of the 19th Judicial District Court in East Baton Rouge Parish. He held that position until 2013 when Wayne, his Wife Tareka, and their two sons Wayne III and David II moved to Metro Atlanta where he has since worked for a handful of boutique firms specializing in family law and personal injury. Since 2018, he has been with the law firm of Kenneth Southall, PC in downtown Atlanta specializing in personal injury recovery. He plans to start his own firm in Atlanta.

While "Uncle Buck" was known on the Yard for participating in numerous extracurricular activities at Southern, he is most fondly remembered as being elected President of the S.U. Student Government Association in 2003. His election was particularly of note because Wayne is the first white student to be elected SGA President not only of Southern University, but of any HBCU ever. Wayne remains active today as a Lifetime Member of the Southern University Alumni Federation, and is an active member of both the Metro Atlanta Chapter as well as the Past Presidents Alliance Chapter.

Growing up in the Creole traditions of New Orleans, Wayne "Uncle Buck" Haydin is an award-winning cook, poet, DJ, and musician. He and his family are devout Roman Catholics, and Wayne is an avid fan of his Southern University Jaguars, the New Orleans Saints, and Atlanta United FC.

SHAQUILLE DILLON

HBCUs at First Sight
Shaquille Dillon

My experience at Southern University and Agricultural & Mechanical College in Baton Rouge, Louisiana, was a transformative journey replete with growth, empowerment, and a deep sense of belonging. It afforded me the opportunity to gain the knowledge I needed to successfully disrupt the space that I would eventually occupy as a higher education administrator at Historically Black Colleges and Universities.

Having grown up less than 100 miles away in Franklinton, Louisiana, one would assume that I was already familiar with the nation's only historically black system of higher education. But that was not the case. I was not born when one of my relatives, Mechelle Martin, who wore the coveted crown of Miss Southern University 1984, attended Southern. I became familiar with the HBCU experience by watching the Bayou Classic each year on television, and, in 2007 as a high school junior, attending homecoming with Ms. Jackie Tate, the late Ms. Cathy Cotton, two of my friends' moms, and the late Mr. W.L. Johnson; it all expanded my horizon on HBCUs.

It didn't take long for me to realize that Southern University was my college of choice, despite the pushback I received from my high school counselors who fare better at a predominantly white institution (PWI). Fortunately for me, my experience and subsequent degree from Southern University proved them wrong. Nowhere else could I have thrived in such a vibrant cultural environment that celebrated the African-American heritage and allowed me to engage in events and activities that amplified not only my voice but the voices of my peers. We were able to better understand our rich and storied history and connect spiritually with our ancestry. It is true, as

Maya Angelou said, "If you don't know where you've come from, you don't know where you are going." The opportunities SU afforded me, allowed me to deepen my connection to my roots and instill in me a sense of pride, respect, and resilience for my forefathers.

I entered Southern University in the fall of 2009, scared and lost, but ready to take on a world that was different from anything I had ever known. However, it was soon after that I found my why and a passion for politics and higher education. I majored in Political Science and became heavily involved in student leadership. I had the pleasure of serving as Sophomore Class President, Men's Federation President, Collegiate 100 Black Men President, a Jaguar Ambassador, and I held numerous other leadership positions. Among my many memorable honors was the opportunities to canvas for President Obama during his second presidential campaign and to attend the National Association of Student Affairs Professions Student Leadership Institute in 2013.

During my matriculation, I grew personally, professionally, spiritually, and emotionally. The faculty and staff oftentimes went above and beyond their ascribed titles and scope of duties to provide meaningful and life-changing assistance to students who found themselves treading in unfamiliar waters. Whether it was a family, a personal situation, or understanding the complexities of coursework, there was always someone there to give a listening ear and a sympathetic shoulder. The strong sense of family that permeated the campus was authentic and could never be duplicated at a PWI, despite its national ranking. The Southern University community was a fine-tuned network of students, faculty, and staff who were sincerely committed to the success of all students.

I can attest to the times when our classrooms became spontaneous platforms for open and honest dialogue and critical thinking. We freely discussed those actions and events that changed the landscape of our nation and the African-American culture. We were no longer spectators sitting on the sidelines and watching the confluence of politics, religion, crime, and other influences forever change the course of our country. Instead, we were encouraged to become problem solvers and impactful contributors to our own future success. I thank God for the instructors who poured into me; the late Dr. Troy Allen, the late Dr. Ruby Jean Simms, Dr. Xavier Hoy, Dr. Leslie Taylor Grover, and Dr. Samuel Albert, who pushed me to do more and become more.

After graduating, I took more than my degree with me. I took a persona that was confident, more culturally aware, and socially conscious. I took with me the aspirations and successes of the thousands of alumni who had gone before me. Their endeavors inspired me to be the best person that I could be. I took with me a renewed sense of pride in the importance of unapologetically being my authentic self in every situation. Southern University taught me the realization that I am enough.

Ironically, I began my professional career at Southern University as an Admissions Recruiter under the Division of Student Affairs and Enrollment Management. As such, I had the opportunity to travel throughout the country recruiting the best and brightest students to Jaguar Nation. For me, it was a job; but for the students I recruited, it was life-changing. When I think about graduates such as LaDonte Lotts, Darby Smith, Anthony Kenney, and my little cousin Destiny Ausmer, I see my God-given purpose fulfilled. SU also allowed me to participate in a marketing and rebranding campaign that effectively enhanced our recruiting efforts.

After leaving Southern University, I accepted the position of Executive Director of Student Life at Wiley College in Marshall, Texas, where I was later promoted to Executive Director of Enrollment Management. Understanding how to recruit and retain students at HBCUs became my focus. I sought innovative ways to introduce intelligent, yet marginalized, Black students to the HBCU experience. That was easy for me because that mirrored my own journey.

As the professional job opportunities increased, so did my successes. After being named Executive Director of Enrollment Services at Tennessee State University, we realized an unprecedented 117% increase in first-time freshmen enrollment. I addressed a critical need by establishing a freshman male mentorship program and the creation of the Build Institute What was designed as a six-week leadership development program became a six-month institute. Build Institute focused on professional development, leadership, principles of manhood, mental health, and vulnerability, among other things. I was blessed to lead 43 freshmen males that were selected amongst the largest freshman class in the university's history. These gentlemen continue to make me proud. We built that institute brick by brick, and I count it as one of my greatest professional accomplishments. Also, my mentees Chandler Cotton, Davin Latiker, Rick Myrie, and Erik Alston have played a major influence on mentoring at HBCUs.

I was recently tapped by one of my mentors, Dr. Melva K. Wallace, to serve as Vice President of Marketing, Strategy, Impact, and Innovation at Huston-Tillotson University, Austin's first institution of higher education and its only HBCU. Dr. Melva K. Wallace, Dr. Brandon K. Dumas, and TaMarlon T. Carter are not only my mentors but they helped to influence my leadership style and to shape my outlook on life. I am eternally grateful to them and all who have poured into my life as a professional and individual.

My professional career has been, and always will be, dedicated to ensuring that our Historically Black Colleges and Universities continue to thrive and remain relevant and accessible for generations of African Americans who, like me, want to be the change that we desire to see in this world.

About Shaquille Dillon

Shaquille K. Dillon serves as the Inaugural Vice President for Marketing, Strategy, Impact, and Innovation at Huston-Tillotson University, where he was responsible for planning, developing, managing, and administering programs and strategies that supports the strategic plan, missions and vision of the university. Additionally, he develops and implements a comprehensive plan to recruit, retain, and serve a vibrant and diverse student body, faculty, and staff.

Dillon has a record of accomplishments and holds more than nine years of experience in higher education administration. Dillon holds two academic degrees: Bachelor of Arts in Political Science - 2013 and a Masters of Public Administration - 2019 from Southern University and Agricultural & Mechanical College and is currently pursuing a Doctorate of Philosophy in Urban Higher Education from Jackson State University.

His leadership has been characterized by great gains, transformational leadership and a momentum of progress and innovation. Prior to being named Vice President of Marketing, Strategy, Impact, and Innovation, he served at Executive Director of Enrollment Services at Tennessee State University. Prior to serving at TSU, he served at Wiley College and Southern University and A&M College.

Although he has earned many honors and recognitions for his work and service, a defining moment in his career was being overwhelmingly voted as Male Advisor of the Year for three consecutive years at the National Association of Student Affairs Professionals Student Leadership Institute (NASAP SLI). Dillon was also selected as HBCU Buzz Top 30 Under 30 - 2017, Alpha Phi

Alpha Fraternity, Inc. Louisiana District Alumni Brother of the Year -2018, and many more.

Dillon's personal and professional achievements have been remarkable, but it is the commitment to excellence and seriousness of purpose he brings to every endeavor he undertakes, that is most impressive. He is active in many educational, social and civic organizations and also a new Life Member for the Southern University Alumni Federation. He defines himself as a disruptive leader, mentor, HBCU advocate, and a lifelong learner.

JASMINE SMUTHERMAN

The Life of a Dreamer
Jasmine Smutherman

As I sit here and reflect on the impact Southern University and A&M College had on my life's trajectory, it would be remiss of me to not acknowledge the moments that lead me to make one of the most life- altering decisions I've ever made. Although I stepped foot on Southern University's soil twenty years ago, the journey and introduction to my HBCU started well beyond that.

When I was a young girl, my attendance in church was very imperative. I would be there at least three days out of the week for choir rehearsal, bible study, praise dance, bible drill, and Sunday service. I had many mentors, teachers, and a solid village that made a huge impact on some of the decisions I would later make in my life. I was surrounded by a village of people that constantly challenged me to strive for anything my heart desired. Church is where I found my voice and began singing on stage. It was where I felt the most comfortable and where I developed some of my life-long friendships. It felt like home most of the time because so much time was spent there. I could look around and see people that looked like me and that had similar beliefs as me.

What I didn't realize growing up, was that I was being groomed for a future I could've never foreseen for myself, had it not been for the impact of my church and the members that attended. My church would arrange college tours to schools that were local as well as colleges that were out of state. I have vivid memories of us commuting in the church bus and touring several college campuses with my peers. Those college tours were preparing me for a promising future. A future that was bright and full of endless possibilities. There were several Southern University Alumni that attended my church and proudly represented every time they had the opportunity to do so.

My very first introduction to Southern University was when a member of my church gave my parents tickets to the Bayou Classic. I never could've imagined what that experience would be like, nor did I know the influence and magnitude it would have on my decision to attend years later. I had never witnessed or experienced anything like it before. The marching band, cheerleaders, Dancing Dolls, school pride, chants, battle of the bands, Greek representation, and all of the likeness and positivity that surrounded me, ignited an excitement and thrill that was indescribable. I knew then that I wanted to be attached to that feeling forever. My mind was made up and when it was time for me to decide on the college that I would attend, I didn't need to look any further. Bayou Classic turned into an annual family trip that my parents committed to every November until my acceptance as a student at Southern University.

From elementary all the way up to high school, I attended predominantly white schools. Being exposed to a world that was foreign to me and completely different from what I was accustomed to, blew my mind. I always dreamed of attending a school where I wasn't the minority. I wanted to cheer on a squad where my teammates and coach looked like me. One thing that I noticed while attending the games at the Bayou Classic, was the cheerleaders and their level of skill while tumbling, stunting, and overall technicality in their style of cheer. It was relatable and mirrored the technique and skill that I knew from a competition standpoint. I was in awe of the familiarity and wanted to know more about this award- winning cheerleading squad. I was so intrigued by the diversity of the team that my interest grew stronger. I had an additional element that helped solidify my decision to attend Southern University. Once it was crystal clear what college I wanted to attend, my parents drove to Louisiana so that I could actually tour the campus. Entering into a new world that was completely different for this shy and somewhat sheltered girl was going to be an adventure and force me to get out of my comfort zone. This was an opportunity to be bold, independent, and courageous. I now had a say on where I wanted to receive my education.

My matriculation began at Southern University Fall 2003, where I majored in Psychology. I loved the intimate setting of the classrooms and the relationships and bonds that were created between professors and students. My love for Psychology developed even more because the professors not only taught the students European Psychology but introduced the importance of African American Psychology and studies.

Wednesdays on campus were a holiday. We called it, "Pretty Wednesday!" It was an opportunity to wear your best and gather with friends between classes in the Student Union. Deciding what outfit to wear in advance was an intentional act, and something that we looked forward to every Wednesday. Never in my life did I anticipate walking to class in heels so effortlessly that it became the norm. There was always something to look forward to on campus from pageants to fashion shows, and programs put on by various organizations.

As a cheerleader on campus, we worked out in the morning before class, and had practice every evening. The amount of structure and discipline that was required of us through our workout regimen daily, taught us the importance of consistency and dedication. Our coach made sure that there was a healthy balance of fun and hard work. My cheer family was my family away from home. When we would travel for away games, it was a requirement for us to take head scarfs off when exiting the bus and entering a building. We were taught to always look presentable because we proudly represented Southern University. The games felt electrifying as we danced to the music and performed for the crowd. From start to finish there was an adrenaline rush.

My last year on campus I decided to run for Miss Southern University. All of my involvement on campus prepared me for the moment that would change my life forever. I was the only non-Greek candidate at the time that I ran for Miss Southern, which was a little intimidating. Campaigning consisted of sending out sponsorship letters to friends and loved ones for financial support. As well as ordering visually pleasing campaign material for students to see as they walked the yard, walking from dorms to campus apartments, knocking on doors to talk to students and passing out campaign material with my team. We had something similar to political debates and a pageant where we showcased our talents. The day the student body voted for me to be the 77th Miss Southern University, was the best day of my life. It surpassed any achievement I had ever accomplished.

During the Fall semester of 2007, I became a proud member of Alpha Kappa Alpha Sorority, Incorporated. I'm so grateful for the experience and my sisters that I gained through the process. We are forever connected, One body, fifty-nine parts.

My HBCU experience molded me into the person that I am today because it taught me to go after anything that I put my mind to. My diverse upbringing allowed me to be able to adapt in different facets of my life. Southern University continues to create spaces for me to show up and continue my legacy through my involvement with the Southern University Queen's Society and the SU Alumni Cheerleader organization. My HBCU connected me with some of my lifelong friends and mentors that helped me along the way. I'm so thankful for this opportunity to share my story and the journey that got me where I am today.

About Jasmine Smutherman

Jasmine Smutherman is from Rowlett, Texas. She began her matriculation at Southern University and A&M College in the fall of 2003, declaring a major in Psychology. She had the honor of representing the student body as the 77th Miss Southern University and A&M College. She is also a member of the illustrious organization, Alpha Kappa Alpha Sorority Incorporated.

She resides in Atlanta, Georgia where she began her career ten years ago as a flight attendant for Delta Airlines. Smutherman is New York based and primarily fly's sports charters. She proudly serves as the "Flight Leader" for the New York Yankees Major League Baseball team, flying the team all over the world during their regular season. She also flies 28 NBA teams and 10 NHL teams. When she's not keeping busy with her career, you can find her traveling during her leisure time to different destinations domestically and internationally.

ERICA ROGERS

The Legacy Continues
Erica Rogers

Southern University has always run deep in my blood! I am a generational Jag, so my love for the blue and gold started at a very young age. As a young girl, and all through my teenage years, I remember the excitement of being at Mumford Stadium very early in the morning handing out Allstate promotional materials with my aunt to earn my ticket to the football games. The exhilaration and excitement of the modern day music, RV camps parked out for miles spanning as far as my eyes could see with the aroma of down home southern cooking and barbecue plates lined up on every table we passed; it felt like a family reunion. To see so many beautiful black faces, hearing laughs and joyful banter always brought my spirit to a happy place. The motorcyclists, the antique cars with big shiny rims playing the latest Cash Money, Lil Boosie, and Lil Weebie hits brought more excitement to onlookers as everyone who knew the songs rapped the lyrics word for word.

And then, at 5:00 pm, my cousin and I would receive our tickets and walk to the game full of confidence with the latest and flyest sneakers as well as our coordinated outfits that we planned all week long. We barely watched the game, it was all about socializing and halftime. The band, the dancing dolls, and the food! The family dynamic of the Jaguar nation and the exciting times at Mumford were two integral factors that led me to my decision of becoming a Jaguar. It was no question that Southern University would be my choice for higher education and to prepare me for the life ahead.

Freshman week, the celebrations started as the bright-eyed, bushy-tailed students moved onto campus and received flyers to all of the fraternity and sorority back-to-school parties. Freshman week was my first taste of independence and an opportunity for me to chart my own course and do it exactly how I wanted. The first week was surreal! The energy of a new chapter and the glory of autonomy pulled me right in. Riding around campus in my new, silver mercury cougar, taking all the action in, and getting dressed up every night partying like I've never experienced gave me a rush of anticipation about how fun this life could really be. The Kappa Luau is one party that every Jag alumni can agree was the most highly anticipated. The Greeks coming together to welcome the newbies to their new life at Southern University. During that week, the older guys from around Baton Rouge would visit and scope out the new freshman on campus. It was quite impressive for a guy doused in cologne, with a nice car, bumping the newest music with a fresh haircut to pull up and talk.

Although the first week was led with excitement, it was embedded in the students that we hold a space in society and our voices were loud enough to continue to push the needle further for more black stories of achievements, leadership and productivity to be told. Student life at Southern University was very unique. The long days at registration to get our billing statements stamped set me on my path of resilience which I cherish as the hallmark of being initiated into the HBCU family and a part of a very distinct and rich culture. The first week of school and throughout my college days, I met friends that turned into family. I built the grit that came with the new onset of independence, self-awareness and autonomy. I grew aware of how blessed I was to be set on a course of greatness and a part of the HBCU legacy. My days at Southern, and the life experiences I endured along the way, were building blocks to my character and how I show up in society today. From campus conversations, to yearly student elections, to being a member of the Beta Psi chapter of Alpha Kappa Alpha Sorority, Inc.- all played a part in the confidence I have in my voice being heard and the acknowledgement of the responsibility that I have to be a voice for the voiceless.

Our professors were key, they made sure to orient us on the responsibility we had of achieving scholastic greatness. My professors were so influential in my life and an integral part of my success today. They were parent figures away from home that cared about our well-being and success. If you slipped, they helped you up while instilling the importance of integrity and accountability. Accountability and integrity were profound tools given to me early on in my higher education tenure that is foundational in my success as a nurse. The rigors of the nursing curriculum and hours of studying made the togetherness of the nursing students grow stronger. I am very proud of my success as a nurse and finding balance in God, self and community during my time in nursing school.

Southern University Nursing school not only provided a top tier education and prepared me for world health challenges but instilled in me the importance of community action and global health which led me to where I am now as a global health humanitarian and founder of Braveheart Foundation. Braveheart Foundation is a global missions organization recruiting nurses and other health professionals to travel to the hard-to-reach villages in Uganda, East Africa, and to volunteer time and provide resources to meet the needs of the health disparities that have long been eradicated in the United States. If I had not been exposed to health advocacy, community action, and global health challenges, the organization would not have been a thought.

Braveheart has recruited several Southern University nursing alumni to experience the journey and pay forward the fruit of our upbringing and education. It has been my highest honor to lead Southern University alumni students on such an impactful journey. Since the inception of Braveheart in 2014, over 7000 Ugandans have received free healthcare during the yearly medical mission and the continuum of sustainable health programs. I am very proud of the legacy that I am building that started with my decision to be a part of the Southern University family, the mighty blue and gold.

About Erica Rogers

Erica Rogers is the founder of Braveheart Foundation and a 14-year tenured registered nurse pursuing a Masters Degree in Public Health and Tropical Medicine at Tulane University. The Southern University graduate is a 2021 honoree of the City Business "Health Care Hero Award". Erica is currently working on the frontlines in Intensive Care Units with the New York City Health and Hospital Corporation while using her expertise in covid-19 mitigation to serve as one the hospital corporation's covid-19 vaccine ambassadors. Erica worked diligently during the early phases of the pandemic in multiple ICUs in the New Orleans area advocating and fighting for patients attacked with the invisible enemy covid-19. Erica and other frontline and military workers were recognized for heroism during the pandemic by the President and Dr. Biden at the 2021 Annual White House Fourth of July celebration.

Erica started a career at Houston's MD Anderson Cancer Center in 2008. Driven by the quote, "Compassion is the highest level of intellect", Erica loved her job right away, but soon became interested in venturing "outside the walls of the hospital" to participate in community outreach work. After developing a close and lasting relationship with a patient in cancer treatment, she understood what was tugging at her heartstrings – she knew that she could be doing more.

Braveheart, was created as a peer-to-peer support system that helped patients and their families cope with the process of cancer treatment. The project's success inspired her to pursue similar endeavors on a larger scale. In 2014, relocating back to Louisiana with plans to embark on a mission trip to Africa she joined a small group of clinicians in Uganda, providing essential medical care to dozens of people. After that trip, Braveheart became a worldwide mission. Braveheart has a mission to promote health education, equitable health services, and sustainable health programming to underserved and marginalized communities worldwide. Acute medical, vision, dental, women's health, and podiatry are the specialties that are provided in the free medical clinics.

Since the inception of Braveheart in 2014, over seven thousand villagers have been impacted with free health services during the annual medical missions. Braveheart foundation uses minimal funding and resources to impact many by providing mass drug administration and in-depth health education in the most desolate villages of Uganda. Braveheart has a partnership with Smiling Hearts orphanage in Lake Buyonyi, Uganda. Braveheart supplies the orphanage with a yearly supply of medications in the kiddie pharmacy while also providing yearly well-kid health check-ups, malaria, dental and vision screening with necessary treatment. In March 2019, the world shifted as we faced the deadly covid-19 pandemic. Braveheart was unable to return to Uganda during this time.

The organization took a quick pivot by going into communities to build capacity and bring awareness to the available resources around Louisiana that provide education and treatments that are geared towards mitigating the health disparities linked to the high mortality rate from covid-19. Education and awareness were brought to unreachable, land-locked and hard-hit communities in different parts of Louisiana. Braveheart Foundation founded the "Krewe of Vax" Vaccination Parade. The vision for the "vaccination parade" campaign is to promote equitable widespread dissemination of the covid-19 vaccine to help mitigate the rapid transmission of the virus in vulnerable populations. The vaccination parade mission was founded with a goal to bring joy and anticipation for a safe return of Mardi Gras back to Louisiana while making a record milestone impact by educating and administering vaccinations to communities in Louisiana.

Braveheart also focuses on educating businesses, educational and governmental leaders on covid-19 safe protocols for gatherings, events, and safe schooling through urging the importance of testing. In the aftermath of Hurricane Ida (2021), Braveheart immediately put boots on the ground to help with relief efforts in hardest hit areas, one of which is Erica's home town of Laplace, Louisiana. The team partnered with local government and facilitated a "Catastrophe Can't Stop Us" tour which was drive-through events distributing much needed household items and hot meals while offering encouragement for hope in a dignified recovery as residents start to rebuild their homes and lives.

During this time, programming was curated to protect the devastated areas environmental health and economic sustainability. Braveheart led a "Clean Sweep" initiative that resulted in 240 tons of trash collected in St. John Parish. Other initiatives such as economic stimulus payments to elderly residents and small business micro grant programs met immediate economic needs of the communities served. The initiatives garnered much success which catapulted Braveheart to facilitate many more mass distributions and donations throughout the devastated areas in Lafourche and Terrebonne Parishes.

Erica is recipient of the 2019 "Millennial Healthcare Award" presented by The Spears Group and New Orleans Business Alliance, "The 2019 Champion for Change Award" presented by the Crescent City Links, "The 2019 Great 100 Nurse of Louisiana Honoree", and an appointed subcommittee member on Governor John Bel Edwards COVID-19 Health Equity task force providing recommendations for mitigating the spread of COVID-19 in the jails and prison systems throughout Louisiana. Other affiliations are 2019 cohort for "Emerging Philanthropists of New Orleans", New Leaders Council 2020 cohort fellow, 2021 cohort fellow for New Orleans Regional Leadership Institute and a member of the New Orleans Citizen Diplomacy Council. A proclamation was presented by St. John Parish former Parish President (Natalie Robottom) in January 2020 in recognition of the work of Braveheart Foundation. Braveheart's medical team plans to return to Uganda in July 2022 for the first time since the Covid-19 pandemic.

STACI JACKSON

Dancing to the Beat of My Own Drum
Staci Jackson

Where do I begin?

It's not often you're blessed with the opportunity to relive some of the best moments of your life in this fashion.

SU has shaped the woman I am today; it's a love very dear to my heart. Choosing Southern University and A&M College was, by far, one of the best decisions I've ever made... and I'll tell you why.

Hi! I'm Staci Jackson, a small-town girl from the beautiful Hammond, Louisiana... of Tangipahoa, Parish. The only daughter of three children and the youngest in the family. The baby girl. So, you would imagine my life growing up was pretty much rainbows and butterflies most of the time, right? You know... the good ol' days. I was a highly sensitive child... introverted yet extroverted, if you know what I mean. Shy in some regards and assertive in others. However, I do remember being very touched by music, movies, and art as a young girl. Oftentimes, they would quickly bring me to tears. That's how I knew I was a little different, or, as my mom says, unique. My two older brothers were supreme athletes, so that made me the princess of the house but also tough as nails. They would challenge me and teach me how to do it all. My brothers knew I would have to toughen up for the world ahead.

My beautiful, hardworking, supportive parents ensured I would have options later on in life, so they insisted on putting me in everything... from dance, gymnastics, basketball, baseball, and cheerleading. I started at the age of three, and, it's safe to say, I was extremely busy and structured yet very fulfilled. They truly believed it'd all be worth it in the long run. They were right. It was then that

I realized how determined I was. Anything that was placed before me was executed to the best of my ability. They instilled excellence from the beginning, and their expectations of me have always been high—Thank you, both, for pushing me to my highest potential and loving me unconditionally. I love you, Mom & Dad!!

The year was 2005, and I remember it like it was yesterday. I graduated from Hammond High with honors and tons of new knowledge and a newfound confidence ready to conquer the world. I was going to my favorite HBCU, Southern University, and, like any eighteen-year-old, I thought I knew everything I needed to know about finally being an "adult." Little did I know, the journey I was about to embark on was unlike any of my expectations. The years to follow truly were some of the most amazing years of my life.

Day one at Southern University was a day to remember. If you know SU, you know the registration process is uniquely designed and can be a social event of its own. In those precious moments, I met the most incredible individuals, and we were all just figuring it out together. Initially, my main focus was on continuing my passion for dance. Prior to enrolling, I dreamed of becoming a Fabulous Dancing Doll, and I studied them endlessly. I knew I wanted to be a part of this incredible dance team since I saw them perform for the first time at a Bayou Classic in 2000. It was love at first sight!!

However, God had other plans for me.

After auditioning my freshman year, I did not make the team and had to decide whether dancing was even going to be an option for me that semester. This was very discouraging for me at the time because dancing was my life and making that squad was important to me. Then, God answered my prayer! Shortly after, I was informed about another dance team's audition that was happening a couple of days later; they were the Gold n Bluez. They are the official basketball dance team for the university. One of my very best friends and I decided to try out together, and we both made it! Talk about excitement! We were over the moon. Being a part of "GNB" was the icing on the cake. The Gold N Bluez dance team was a dancer's dream. We traveled, performed at pep rallies and basketball games, competed with other amazing teams, and were able to dance to our favorite songs! Those moments will forever be vivid in my mind. I'm grateful for that team. I was even captain of the team for a year. I got the chance to dance alongside the most beautiful and gifted dancers from all over. It was amazing!

After three phenomenal years on Gold N Bluez. I decided to audition again for the Fabulous Dancing Dolls. Being a part of that dance team was still a goal of mine, and I'm so happy I did. Another goal and aspiration of mine was accomplished! God is so great! I was now a part of the Human Jukebox and all the magic that entails. The Blueprint; as some would call it. Southern University is known globally for the incredible talent the band has always possessed. Therefore, it was a complete honor to be added to that list. My two years as a Dancing Doll flew by and felt like a dream come true. It was then that I felt compelled to try out for the New Orleans Saints Cheerleading Team. I researched the audition dates, made sure I met all the requirements, and tried my best! Luckily, my best was good enough! I was an official NFL Cheerleader, and my family and I were beyond thrilled. The football games, practices, and appearances kept my schedule full, but it was the moment of a lifetime, and I made it happen. Even while working, commuting, and finishing school. An opportunity like this can't ever be taken for granted.

Sometimes, we forget the sacrifice it takes to be involved in activities other than class-related work. Being able to juggle my academics while dancing wasn't always easy. It was hard work. I majored in Therapeutic Recreation, which is truly everything I'm about. Dancing is very therapeutic and healing for so many people. It was a major that included sports as well; I was in my element. However, there were moments when I felt overloaded. Time management is extremely imperative in order to be successful at any university. Not getting distracted from what's important was the challenge. Staying on top. There were times when my friends and I stayed up too late or partied the night before... but had class the next day. We soon realized those little bad habits needed to be broken. I was then able to prioritize my school work and dance schedule so that I could be successful in both areas.

I must say... It was all a huge balancing act.

When it comes to the friendships I've gained over my college years... the bonds are forever and mean so much to me. Walking to class, Pretty Wednesdays, the circle; we were everywhere together. These are the individuals that looked out for me when I had no one else. I don't think people realize this, but... our freshmen year was the year Hurricane Katrina did so much damage to the surrounding communities of Louisiana. Our world was shaken up a bit, and we were all we had. There was no electricity for a while, flooding in some areas, no telephone service, we couldn't call home, it was a bit much. However, it made our bonds that much stronger. Even after graduating, the relationships continued and have grown deeper. We still try to spend time together whenever we can. Friends turn into family at Southern University.

Life after SU has been quite eventful. I am now a mother to a beautiful 11-year-old. Natalie is her name, and she is the apple of my eye. Being her mom is my highest accomplishment and blessing thus far. As you can imagine, things are much different than they were during college. True responsibilities have kicked in, and adulthood is adulting. But I still find time to do the things that I love, and that helps tremendously.

I'm currently teaching physical education and performing arts to a brilliant group of kids, and they are so precious and keep me on my toes. I also started a business, Staci J. & Co., where I extend my performing arts services to individuals seeking fitness and dance training. I'm a performer as well and work with several corporate production companies around Louisiana. It's been busy, but I'm grateful for each blessing. Acting and music have also been added to my creative palette. Songwriting comes easy to me, and I love to sing and create beautiful music. I've been a part of so many spectacular films, television shows, and commercials. Again, all of these bring me great joy and fulfillment. I have finally found my purpose and am ready to share it with the world. So you may ask yourself, what's next for Staci?

It's still being written.

About Staci Jackson

Staci Jackson is from Hammond, Louisiana of Tangipahoa Parish. She is many things but to sum it all up … Staci is an artist, a musician, an actress, a model, a mother … and a dancer but the list goes on and on. She likes to do it all, she believes you are your only limit.

Thirty-four glorious years of competitive dance training in all styles of dance and professional work have filled Ms. Jackson's years with so much passion, fulfillment and major success. But of course, striving to make her family proud while trying to balance & maintain all that is placed before her is not always easy. Staci is thankful for God's grace and mercy. He guided her through.

Ms. Jackson choose Southern University & A&M College simply because it was Southern University and she is so glad she made that choice!!

The Jaguar Nation is and will always be the standard for HBCU's around the world. Staci had the honor of dancing alongside the most beautiful and talented performers in sold out stadiums … travel with the Human Jukebox, cheer on our amazing sports teams and meet so many brilliant individuals along the way. Friendships turn into family at Southern U and she will cherish the memories she made there forever.

And as for life after SU … it's still being written …

IRONE ROUSSELL

Forever Family
Irone Roussell

The year is 2006, and, in a faint distance, a growing chant fills the atmosphere. "AAYYYYYE – OH!.....AYYYYYEEEE OH!" The sounds of snare drums rip through the stadium media. As the volume grow increasingly louder, the unlikeliest of phenomena catches my eye as the poster child for what seemed to be the most intimidating and massive army ever assembled. For the first time, I laid my eyes on the Fabulous Dancing Dolls; Fierce but Graceful, Strong but Sensual! The looming chants carry on as the band continues to pour through Gate 9, and, suddenly, the drum major blows his whistle. The band snaps their horns up, and they begin marching through the stadium playing "Get Your Number" by Mariah Carey. At this very moment, I was sold! I knew I had to be a part of the Human Jukebox.

The sway of the instruments and their continuous pouring out of an unrelenting sound, provided the perfect imagery of what it meant to be a cohesive unit. This was my senior year of high school, and the 2006 SUBR Homecoming Game was my first experience in A.W. Mumford Stadium. I had heard of Southern University, but having the experience first-hand was everything to a 17-year-old kid who just wasn't sure about what his future held. See, I had lost everything the year prior due to the events of Hurricane Katrina. When I say I lost everything, I mean EVERYTHING: hope, ambition, motivation, all of it. I quietly suffered in my circumstances and began to slowly give up on the idea of college; however, the one glimpse of hope I had come by way of Southern University.

Welcome to the Jukebox

In the Summer of 2007, I auditioned for an opportunity to be a part of the Southern University Human Jukebox. During my senior year, I developed a relationship with the former Associate Director of Bands, Mr. Carnell Knighten, and then recently retired Director of Bands, Dr. Isaac Greggs while I was a part of the Louisiana Leadership Institute Marching Band (LLI). Being a part of Louisiana Leadership had given me a shot at making something greater of my circumstances. These men saw to it that I would have an opportunity to be a part of something as prestigious as the Human Jukebox.

When you say "Southern University," the first thing that comes to mind is "The Human Jukebox" Marching Band. Becoming a member of the best collegiate band program in the country required me to grow out of adolescence, quickly showing me that I had a major duty and responsibility to uphold the "S"tandard of everything that was built before me. It was the best thing that happened to me early in my collegiate career. I learned how to manage my studies, alongside my responsibilities to the band program. The long nights of practice, coupled with having to be timely in completing my coursework only helped me prove to myself that I was suited to be a college student. As cliché as it sounds, staying on top of your work isn't the easiest thing in college. However, being a freshman in the Human Jukebox kept me grounded, with me only having time to focus on the necessities of being a college student.

It is remarkable how things can change so much in a year. I was once a spectator as I looked on in awe of the band, and now I had the honor of being a member of the band program. Being in the band came with a level of exposure I never imagined. From the many home games to traveling to away games, Bayou Classic, Boombox Classic, and other events across the country, I had done enough in one semester to eclipse my whole high school career. I had never traveled this much before and performed in so many venues. I was just a project kid and had no clue of what was out there in the world for me, but I very quickly learned the importance of quality preparation. It became an innate responsibility to be at the right place, at the right time, with the right equipment ready to concentrate. It was more than just "band practice" as some of the masses believed. We prepared weekly to go to war, and that required every one of the 200+ members to be fully invested in the brand that is the Southern University Human Jukebox. Every practice felt like a performance because we knew that we weren't competing with anyone else, but simply competing with the legacy of the JUKE!

As my college years progressed, I found myself growing as a leader in the band program, thanks to the Director of Bands, Lawrence Jackson (or Mr. J, as we call him.) Being under his tutelage was a huge contribution to my growth as an aspiring Music Educator and Band Director. As a Music Education Major, the daily commitment to being the best in the band room embedded all the principles in which I operate on today in my position as a Music Educator, and band director. It is because of the Southern University Human Jukebox Marching Band that I am in the position to guide and develop my students towards their own potential with hopes of them aspiring to be a part of the Legacy of Southern University.

Greek Life

"Goodwill is the monarch of this house!" are the words that ring loudly in the House of Alpha and the hearts of my brothers. I was fortunate to be chosen for membership into the Beta Sigma Chapter of Alpha Phi Alpha Fraternity, Inc. in the Spring of 2009. Being initiated as a sophomore, I was fortunate to have been chosen above many others which afforded me a lengthy tenure of undergraduate Greek Life experience. I have created countless memories with my fraternal brothers, memories that are growingly vivid with every passing day. Imagine waking up to a call saying, "Hey, ESPN has requested that you guys perform on Sports Nation. It'll be live and Nationally Televised." WHAT??? I never imagined opportunities like this would fall into my lap. I was blessed to perform on a live Nationally televised program, several Bayou Classic Step Shows, be one of the main attractions for Friday night homecoming festivities, the National Alpha Convention, countless step shows across the country. These opportunities don't just come to anyone but are catered to a specific demographic of people who are direct representatives of the school's culture.

As members of Black Greek Letter Organization (BGLO), we are tasked with a huge responsibility to represent the school and community on a much greater stage. We stand on the principles that our founders, brothers, and sisters before us have put in place to serve our communities and be an example for all to follow. The misconception that Greek organizations are only about Step shows and Stroll-Offs very often lead incoming students to seek these organizations for the wrong reasons. We are so much more to Southern University and the communities that surround us. We provide education outside of the classroom to our peers, motivate and inspire grade school students to aim higher when it comes to their academic success, pay homage, and give back to our elders who came before us and paved the way, among so many other ways that we impact the world.

My time as an undergraduate member has been fueled by all the constant opportunities to expand my network within the BGLOs at SU, with brothers from other chapters, as well as other fraternities and sororities at other schools. Being able to travel to other universities and have other chapters at other schools show love to you as if they've known you their whole life, was one of my favorite aspects of college life because the notoriety of Southern University Greeks was greater than I initially knew. When you said your chapter name people already knew, THAT'S SOUTHERN! This same group of people have been there for me emotionally, financially, have supported my business endeavors, life ventures, and in many other countless ways. We all share a love for SU and belong to an elite company of Southernites.

The SU Family

Of Course, College is about academia first, but what Southern University has afforded me is a support system of mentors and peers that WANT to see me succeed beyond the classroom. I can still call my professors today and inquire about whatever resources that I may need to excel. I can call my peers, message them on social media, ask for their support, and receive their blessings in the name of our beloved University. These people are LIFETIME gifts; past, present, and future Southernites that will ultimately be there to provide opportunities should you need them. Upon graduation, I was able to find a teaching job in my field in JANUARY, the middle of the school year, largely in part to the alumni of my beloved university. When we say "DEFENDERS OF THE GOLD AND BLUE," we stand on the notion that SU is not just a system of schools in Louisiana, but a World-Wide Campus. Our ties extend beyond the yard, beyond "The Hump", beyond A.W. Mumford stadium, T.T. Allain, Debose Music Hall, U.S. Jones Hall, J.S. Jones Hall, Totty and Shade Hall, "The Circle, The MiniDome. We are a family where we find ourselves settled, and that is what I believe is the greatest asset that SU has afforded me, a FAMILY. I know one thing is guaranteed no matter where I am: wherever there is an "S," there is "YOU"! Go Jags!!

About Irone Roussell

Irone E. Roussell is a High School Educator, Band Director, Entrepreneur, and Motivational Speaker, serving his community in every way possible. As a Native of New Orleans, Louisiana, music has always innately been a part of his culture and upbringing. He is a two-time Graduate of Southern University and A&M College, with a bachelor's degree in music education and a master's degree in educational leadership. While at Southern University, Irone was a member of the World-Renowned Human Jukebox Marching Band, and a Spring 2009 Initiate of the Beta Sigma Chapter of Alpha Phi Alpha Fraternity, Inc. He is also an Honorary Member of the Delta Psi Chapter of Kappa Kappa Psi National Honorary Band Fraternity at Prairie View A&M University.

Being a perfect example of "Your Plan vs God's Plan", he is thriving as a profound Educator in the Dallas Independent School District, having formerly served as an educator in East Baton Rouge Parish Schools. Having his mother as his first teacher set the precedent for him possessing the necessary elements to guide and instruct young individuals into their greatness.

In his 9 Years as a Band Director and Educator, Irone has consistently achieved and excelled, setting the bar high for his students to become accomplished musicians at LMEA District Music Festivals, as well as Region 20 UIL Music Assessments in the state of Texas. He also served on the Director's staff for Louisiana Leadership Institute as a Music Arranger, having performed for events as prestigious as the Presidential Inaugural Parade of 2021. He has seen well over 100+ students off to college and awarded Scholarships to deserving college students through his business "The Flowcus Brand". He remains excited in every way to continue building a brighter future for young people in education, and inspiring future educators to trailblaze in the field of education.

MARK JONES

Let's GEAUX!
Mark Jones

When I left Los Angeles, at the age of eighteen, to enroll at Southern University and A&M College, I felt a mix of apprehension and excitement. Being a city kid moving to the South had its wonders. I was torn between staying home with all my family and friends or leaving my comfort zone to start my journey in a different state.

Gang violence in Los Angeles was impossible to avoid, even if you weren't involved in the street life yourself. It was just the culture in the area I grew up in. Something told me I needed to leave California and explore some place different, and that's exactly what I did.

My college counselor, Ms. Flett, was surprised that I had no intention to apply to any California state schools. With no historically black colleges and universities on the west coast, I was forced, in a way, out of my comfort zone. The only colleges I applied to were HBCUs. Once I told her the reason why I only applied to out of state schools, she completely understood and was determined to get me into the university of my choice!

I ended up getting accepted to about twelve HBCUs. After careful research and consideration, it came down to the final two schools to choose where my new life would begin. It was between Hampton University in Virginia or Southern in Baton Rouge, Louisiana. I remember sitting at the kitchen table back home before I made my choice; my step-dad walked in and told me to make a choice. He just reminded me that whichever school I chose was going to be the right choice, and there was no wrong decision. The ball was in my court. I ended up choosing Southern because I always watched the Bayou Classic on NBC and could feel the energy and pride of the alumni and students through the TV. I wanted to be a part of that! Next thing you know, I arrived for my first day on campus at the jaguar preview.

When I arrived on campus, I didn't know what to expect. The first thing I remember was how hot it was when we stepped off the plane in Baton Rouge. I had always heard of humidity, but I had never really experienced it in real life. Where I'm from, it's hot in the daytime but gets cold at night. This was not the case in Baton Rouge, Louisiana. It's hot in the daytime and still hot at night. To this day, I still haven't adjusted, but I manage.

The Jaguar preview was my introduction to Southern. After that, we finally got through with financial aid. The first place the student tour guides brought us was Mayberry Hall on a Monday. My parents and I stood in line unaware of the dining experience we were about to encounter. Such a strategic move by the tour guides. After we devoured a plate of red beans and rice complimented by a perfectly fried chicken thigh, my parents knew I was going to be in good hands.

Meeting new people has never been hard for me. Within the first week on campus, I already had a crew. My roommate and I shared an interest in basketball, and he took me to hoop on the courts in front of the Old Jones Dorms. Once I established myself on the basketball court, I started meeting all types of people from different states. It was exciting to interact with them. These were all people that looked like me from all around the world who had the same ultimate goal as me. We all were there to get an education. The fact that the university I chose was a safe place where people of color were able to flourish and thrive intrigued me.

Life at Southern was busy, and I had to find ways to manage the stress that came with academic demands, extracurricular activities, and my part-time job. I had to learn to prioritize and balance my time effectively. My first semester of my freshman year, my mom "helped" me with my class schedule. She convinced me to schedule all early classes so I can enjoy the rest of my day. That sounded great at the time because I hadn't experienced on campus living yet and knew nothing about "The Circle" at night time. Needless to say, my second semester schedule looked nothing like my first. Those 8 AM classes were a thing of the past. I had to find balance between school and my new social life. But my determination and discipline paid off, and I graduated on time, with a degree in business, which prepared me for my future endeavors.

While on campus, I wanted to be involved in more activities. Just being a student wasn't enough for me. I'm a very social person and wanted to be a part of something that had real meaning. I ended up working with the women's basketball team as a team manager after I was approached by one of the coaches asking if I would help out with the team when they needed to scrimmage. From there, I was asked to start coming to team practices, then, next thing I know, I was traveling with the team and getting coaching experience. While I was with the team for three seasons, we won two SWAC regular season titles and one SWAC tournament championship.

The experience I had with the women's team inspired me to bring M9 back. M9 is the student section at the basketball games that started long before I got to Southern. I wanted to bring M9 back but needed a way to convince the students to come to the game and bring the energy. I brought the idea to the AD. He approved of my idea and even helped me with sponsorships from Raising Canes and other local businesses. They provided us with giveaways like shirts, cups, mini basketballs, and more.

With all these giveaways I had, I needed a team. I put out the word in the college of Business that the athletic department was looking for eight interns to help out with game day entertainment. To my surprise, many people came out, and I ended up creating the GEAUX TEAM. That's right, the Geaux Team that you see today at basketball games was created by me. It's a great feeling to come back to basketball games and see something I created still going strong.

One of my proudest achievements during my time at Southern was becoming a member of Alpha Phi Alpha Fraternity, Inc. Joining a fraternity was not only an opportunity to bond with like-minded individuals but also a chance to serve our community and contribute to positive change.

As an entrepreneur in the pool industry, I have applied the knowledge I gained from Southern's business school to my business operations, and it has helped me run a successful enterprise. However, the journey wasn't easy, and it wasn't just because of the challenges that come with starting a business. Being a Black business owner comes with its own set of issues, and it has been grounding to use what I learned at Southern to navigate those challenges.

Now, I am proud to have over two million followers on social media, where I share my journey as a social media influencer and a successful Black business owner. Southern University and A&M College was the best decision I could have made as an eighteen-year-old, fresh out of Inglewood, CA. I wouldn't have it any other way.

About Mark Jones

Mark Jones is a successful businessman and entrepreneur who has achieved great success through hard work, dedication, and a strong passion for his craft. Originally from Los Angeles, California, Mark relocated to Louisiana after finishing high school in a quest to start afresh and explore new opportunities.

Starting out with just a dream and a passion for pool maintenance, Mark worked tirelessly to turn his passion into a successful business that has continued to grow in leaps and bounds. Mark's rise to success didn't happen overnight, but it was through his unrelenting and dogged pursuit of excellence that he was able to build his business from the ground up.

Mark's strategy was simple, yet effective – knocking on doors and passing out flyers to get the word out about his burgeoning pool maintenance business. Through years of hard work and dedicated service, Mark has cultivated a reputation as one of the top-rated pool maintenance companies in all of New Orleans.

One of the things that has set Mark apart from other entrepreneurs is his unwavering commitment to his family, who played a pivotal role in his journey. Mark has been married for seven years now and has three beautiful children who have been a constant source of motivation and inspiration to him. He credits his family with believing in him and constantly pushing him to pursue his dreams, despite the many challenges he faced.

Today, Mark is a social media star with over two million followers across various platforms. He is known for his engaging and informative posts on pool maintenance, as well as his educational videos which have helped many homeowners take care of their own pools. His expertise and credibility in the field of pool maintenance have made him the go-to guy for homeowners and businesses in need of reliable pool maintenance services.

While Mark is grateful for the success he has achieved thus far, he still has big ambitions for the future. One of his top priorities is to expand his business to include a pool store that will cater to all the needs of pool owners. His vision is to provide his customers with a one-stop-shop where they can find everything they need to maintain their pools, from cleaning supplies to accessories.

Mark's time at Southern University reinforced his belief in himself and the importance of perseverance in the face of adversity. While he faced many obstacles along the way, he never lost sight of his goals or his unwavering confidence that he could succeed.

Mark Jones is a true testament to the power of hard work, dedication, and perseverance. Through his pioneering spirit and sheer force of will, he has built a thriving business, established himself as a social media influencer, and become a role model to countless people who aim to follow in his footsteps. With his indomitable will and tireless work ethic, there is no doubt that Mark will continue to thrive and achieve even greater heights in the years to come.

EBONEE JONES

Southern: A Generational Journey
Ebonee Jones

In order to understand where you are going, you must understand where you come from. My Southern experience boils down to one thing: a journey. Here's my journey into my love and passion for the GREAT Southern University System.

Journey Before Southern

I dedicate this segment to my late, maternal grandmother, Cora Mae Robinson. She passed right before she could hear the news of my participation in this great project. She is the nucleus of my Southern legacy. In the 60's, my grandmother, and several other students from the Hammond, LA, area, took a dedicated bus commuting to and from Southern University. It was THE school that could educate the masses in our community in that era. In the 80's, my aunt, Carolyn, came to "The Yard," and my mother, Penny, wasn't too far behind in the 80's/90's era. Blessings happen on The Yard, because God destined for my parents, Penny and Eric, to meet, and I became the next generation of the Southern Legacy…

Throughout my childhood, my mother constantly reminisced on the good times at SU. The professors, peers, and personalities, all shaped her views on our prestigious institution. Athletics and engineering shaped my dad's view of SU. As a kid, I got to see our mascot, Lacumba, in her cage with my mom, or travel up I-55 for the Boombox Classic against Jackson State with my dad. By the time I got to the 2000's era, HBCUs and Southern had made their way into film references that immediately piqued my interest! BET's *Black College Tour, College Hill, Drumline, Stomp The Yard, A Different World*, and, surely, *School Daze* stamped my approval of knowing that I'd be enrolling at an HBCU. I would attend Homecoming and the Bayou Classic rooting for SU. God fixed it that Southern would ultimately be my destination as the scholarships and grants gave me my full ride. That was ironic, considering I had every intention of attending another HBCU out-of-state. My bank account thanked me for that later down the road.

Little did I know, my mother was already orchestrating with the late Dr. Beverly Wade, former Dean of Honors College at Southern, for me to be accepted coming from Baton Rouge Magnet High, Class of 2008. I entered the halls of Southern University, in the fall of 2008, as a commuting student in the Delores Margaret Richard Spikes Honors College majoring in Business Management. My friends and family were not far, but Southern opened up a whole new world of experiences and friendships that would soon form for me.

Journey During Southern

To really appreciate the full Southern experience, I truly believe one must matriculate to understand why we support and love SU the way we do. I've been blessed to have several community leaders, faculty, and staff influence me during my time at Southern. Essentially, I didn't know what I wanted to do as a career, but my mom always instilled in me to "get a degree in something I could get a job in." And that is how Business Management became my major of choice. Business was safe, and I later realized companies started considering supply chains as recruiting areas. It was the best decision to make, but my first collegiate goal was to obtain internships. I knew, if I did that, the job opportunities would be greater.

The first thing I learned at Southern is that it's not always what you know, but WHO you know. I tried the internship route on my own with INROADS opportunities my freshman year, and failed. I needed some help and guidance. That's where the SU Office of Career Services helped immensely. I built a relationship with the Director, Tamara Foster-Montgomery, and she constantly groomed and mentored me until my résumé was perfect. The only work experience I had was part-time retail, and it didn't really demonstrate transferable skills that I needed to land the internship of my future career. After Mrs. Montgomery's guidance, I had exactly what I needed to land my first "big girl" opportunity. Career Services and student organizations in the College of Business hosted mock interview sessions and elevator pitches to propel my confidence with recruiters. Finally, in the fall of 2010 and spring of 2011, I interviewed with Johnson and Johnson Company and accepted a 6-month co-op at their Neutrogena location in Los Angeles. This was what I prepared for! I had SU and Louisiana on my shoulders as I journeyed to LA for this opportunity. It was my first true time away from home, but SU prepared me!

After my J&J co-op, the opportunities were endless. But let's back up. There's another element that Southern teaches us all to have under our belt, and that includes our well roundedness in student organizations. Since I was a freshman, I showed my leadership by being an officer with the Alpha Chi Chapter of Phi Beta Lambda Business Fraternity. My chapter advisor and class professor, Lauri Patterson, taught me the overarching life motto: "Closed mouths don't get fed," and it stuck with me! I networked and gained leadership that encouraged me to join other organizations. Black Executive Exchange Program (BEEP), Society for Supply Chain Professionals, and my induction into Beta Gamma Sigma Honors Society were just a few throughout my matriculation.

Another big part of Southern included the conferences we attended. Thurgood Marshall College Fund interviews for their Leadership Conference yearly. In 2012, I was awarded the opportunity to attend in New York and be one of twelve representing SUBR. We even got stuck due to the superstorm, Sandy, that year, but it allowed us extra time to network with the hundreds of other HBCU students nationwide. It was beautiful being in one place where I not only saw Black Excellence, but I got to see other HBCU students just as eager as we were. I learned to exude my HBCU pride in any setting and speak with diction thanks to Dr. Erma Hines' Speech class. The book of Ecclesiastes 9:11 states, "I'm reminded that the race is not given to the swift, but to the one who endures to the end." This became prevalent once I found myself extending graduation in order to pursue the great internship opportunities time allowed. As a result, I ended up with an extended time for my honors thesis, a chance to study abroad in China, and the opportunity to become a Spring 2014 initiate of the Alpha Tau Chapter of Delta Sigma Theta Sorority, Inc. The blessings were innumerable in this season! My time at Southern allotted me the ultimate reward: a job out of college! And, if one wasn't enough, God blessed another company to extend employment to me despite me not even showing interest! Through God's grace, Southern opened the doors that set me on the right pace of life as I now know it!

Journey After Southern

My internship in Dallas, TX awarded me a full-time offer after graduation. The company was flexible with my start date, so I paced myself by finishing my degree in the spring of 2014. Upon graduation, I had to take Strategic Management and work in a group project. That group consisted of myself and my future husband. Now, don't get me wrong, I didn't come to SU to get my M-R-S degree. However, there was something about our "A" project that turned into a beautiful journey. We dated across the Texas/Louisiana state line until we were able to settle in Dallas together as one. Now married, my husband, Carlton L. Jones Jr., and I created our own Southern legacy, Caleb Nasir Jones.

I currently have the opportunity to serve the Southern University Alumni Federation (SUAF) with the Dallas Chapter. Collectively, Dallas Alumni have the opportunity to volunteer with nearly 100 different college fairs and award close to $30K in scholarships to Dallas native students matriculating at Southern. I get the opportunity to serve with other dynamic young alumni and "seasoned" Jags across the Dallas-Fort Worth Metroplex. Nothing is more rewarding than serving as a mentor to our current students, and being a big sister to the "baby jags" on The Yard. Giving our time and money back to Southern is something we get to live out monthly through our local alumni chapter.

I've also been able to impact corporate awareness of HBCUs by being a vocal force on HBCU history through events with my company's Black Employee Resource group (BEN). This afforded me the opportunity to plan, host, and execute several engagement events around Black History Month that featured panel discussions on the HBCU and Divine 9 experiences. My involvement with Southern gained the attention of my then manager, who also happened to be a Southernite. Thanks to my involvement with both career and alumni efforts, SUAF awarded me the Forty Under 40 designation. I'm forever grateful, SU!

Dear Southern, I will forever live gold and bleed blue for you…

About Ebonee Jones

A native of Baton Rouge, Louisiana, Ebonee was fortunate to grow up around the love of Southern University and all Historically Black Colleges & Universities. Ebonee is a third-generation legacy to the Southern tradition and had the privilege to create her own experiences while matriculating at SU.

She attended Southern from 2008-2014 obtaining a Bachelor of Science in Business Management with a concentration in Supply Chain. Her campus involvement ranged from various organizations within the College of Business, Career Service Ambassadors, a feature of "Faces of SU" on YouTube, and last but not least, an initiate into the Alpha Tau Chapter of Delta Sigma Theta Sorority, Inc.

Ebonee was able to create a pathway into her professional career by interning with several Fortune 500 companies such as Johnson & Johnson, Texas Instruments, and Boeing Corporation. Her passion for HBCUs traveled into her professional space with her volunteerism in her company's Black Employee Network employee resource group. From there, Ebonee has managed events around HBCU awareness, and current corporate partnerships around Black History Month.

Ebonee resides in the Dallas-Fort Worth Metroplex where she is married to fellow Southernite classmate Carlton L. Jones, Jr. with their son Caleb Nasir. She continues her involvement with Southern University's Alumni Federation Dallas Chapter as a representation of SU's Young Alumni, and is a Life Member to the Alumni Federation. Throughout the pandemic, Ebonee was nominated for the Cohort Trois of Forty Under 40 Distinguished Recipients within Southern Alumni. Mentorship from the HBCU and female perspectives are huge components to Ebonee's success, and she gives back in her involvement with the Dallas Chapter as a Mentor to current SU students. Someone gave so that Ebonee can now give. "Iron sharpens iron," –Proverbs 27:17

KAYONCA RIGGS

The Resilient Jaguar
Kayonca Riggs

"Kayonca, we can keep your baby girl for your first year of college," my mom said as I shared with her about my full-tuition scholarship from the Honors College of Southern University A&M College. It was a huge decision to make as a teenage mother who had never been away from home. I contemplated, for a few days, how I could make this work. My support team assured me that they would help with my daughter, as I stayed on campus my first year of college. Many of them are Southernites, and they encouraged me to enjoy the college experience. I had a support system, and we had a plan that we were determined to make work!

The summer of 2008 was the first time I set foot onto Southern's Campus. Jaguar Preview gave me an opportunity, before classes began, to test out the college experience for a week. I then convinced myself that I could do it! I could live on campus, focus on my studies, and have peace knowing that my daughter was in great care. I was only an hour away from home, and, in the event I needed to get home unexpectedly, I had an emergency plan.

As I packed for my school year, I grew emotional. Not only was this going to be my first time away from home, but this also would be my first time away from my daughter for such a long period of time. I can vividly remember the day I left home. I hugged my daughter so tight, and, to my surprise, she was emotionally well. She had so much love around her, and that gave me the security I needed to carry on with great courage.

We traveled down Highway 190 East for an hour, and, as we crossed over the hump at Southern University, my new reality started to set in. I was a little nervous about this adjustment, but I began working through my nervousness quickly. I convinced myself to be brave and to remember that, on the other side of this sacrifice, there was a great reward. We parked in front of Totty Hall and began to unload my things. I began to feel a sense of peace knowing that my high school classmates were my suitemates. A feeling of home away from home.

My memories of Southern are very fond moments of time embracing my culture in ways I had never experienced before the yard. I met so many beautiful people from all over the world. In between classes and studying, there was always something we could engage in. The walks to Mayberry or Dunn Cafeteria for lunch and dinner were filled with introductions of getting to know other students on campus. Red beans and rice on Mondays was a highly anticipated Louisiana culinary custom.

I went to my first party off campus, Housequake, and I had such a good time. I was always cautious about the places I visited and the activities I engaged in because the responsible part of me understood I was to take care of my business and to never disappoint my support system that was caring for my daughter.

Then I experienced my first homecoming! That was a week to remember. I saw Plies and Chrisette Michele in concert! I had never seen so many people so proud to be a graduate of Southern University. Today, I completely understand! I experienced so many firsts at my Alma Mater!

In November of 2008, Obama was running for president, and I voted for the first time! The entire campus stayed up all night until it was announced that Obama, our first black president, had won! We celebrated so much. Our hearts were so full of joy. That night, I experienced the celebration of our culture in a way that made me so proud to be BLACK! I remember the song "My President" by Jeezy blaring out of the cars of students riding through campus all night! We danced so much to Baton Rouge's Jig music and New Orleans' bounce songs. It was in that moment of time I knew I found where I could really thrive amongst my people, all while pursuing my education.

As my first semester was coming to an end, I knew Bayou Classic was an event all Southern graduates and students looked forward to attending after Thanksgiving. It was an eventful weekend to enjoy ourselves before the week of finals. My friends and I planned our stay and had a blast! We then had Mardi Gras, Spring Break, and then Finals. My first year of college was very successful. I was so excited to go home for the summer and reunite with my baby girl!

That summer, I worked on a plan to reside off-campus and bring my daughter along. The following years, my life was plagued with many problems that I overcame to complete my degree. Depression and anxiety would pay me a visit very often, but I was so determined to FINISH! I worked hard to secure stability. I managed my finances well, and I made sure to schedule therapy sessions for my mental health. I am forever grateful for my professors, who were invested in making sure I succeeded.

The very last semester of my matriculation was the most difficult, darkest season of my life. I did not care to share what I was experiencing to avoid being pitied. I made sure I organized my time to finish my assignments in advance, so I could have a chance to breathe! I was so overwhelmed with grief and fear that my physical health began to decline. I would whisper to myself through my tears, "Kay we are almost finished! We are almost there!" As my world was crumbling around me, I stayed on task.

I received an unexpected call from my Department Chair. I answered, and she said, "Hello, Kayonca, I have not heard from you in a while. Are you okay?" I cried as I responded. I informed her that I was not okay, and I explained my current state of distress. I was walking that season out alone and was ashamed to share what I was experiencing. She said, "You have passed your Departmental Comps. You just need to complete your graduation application, and I will go to the Registrar's Office and pay for everything." She was extremely sympathetic, and she offered me instant relief! After that call, I took a deep breath and whispered, "Kay we are finished, we did it!" During that season, I did not get to attend my graduation ceremony, but, as soon as I came out of that season, I picked up my degree, and I felt very accomplished.

Out of my suffering, I gained my strength, my tenacity, my will power, and MY DEGREE! I stand firm as a proud Southern Alumnae. My HBCU experience is unparalleled. Now that I am on this side of my degree, I have a community of graduates that support me. We support one another. Southernites take care of each other in our careers and business ventures. I feel so secure knowing that no matter where I go, there is a Southern Alumni Chapter ready to take in one of their own. We are Southern! We are Family! A Place of True Support!

About Kayonca Riggs

Kayonca Riggs is a business woman, a philanthropist, and a successful single mother to her daughter and son. She is a country creole girl from the great city of Opelousas, where she embodied the moral code of being what many call "good people." She received a full-ride honors scholarship from Southern University where she obtained a dual Bachelor's degree in Biology and Psychology. She is the founder of The Risen Queen Foundation and the owner & chief operator of Tavia Botanicals, her plant-based home care line that sponsors women and children survivors of domestic violence. She also volunteers for charities that support children's cancer research. She thrives in the community with her philanthropic efforts for causes that are near and dear to her heart.

Her passion and purpose is centered around motherhood, faith, women empowerment, and financial security. She enjoys making connections with other humanitarians that support one another with the common goal of restoring others emotionally and mentally.

Her personal mission statement: "I want to leave this Earth's realm on E! I want to have touched, helped, and healed everyone I was supposed to. I want to have gone everywhere I was supposed to. I want to have done life with the most amazing people on this planet."

MEGAN DANIELS

She Can Still Do It
Megan Daniels

Back in 1997 I attended my first Bayou Classic (well at least the first that I can remember) and remember seeing the fabulous dancing dolls, the Human jukebox marching band, the Sororities and Fraternities, and thought to myself, "I'm going to that school." A few years later after being selected by my middle school dance coach, I had the opportunity to attend a week-long band and dance camp at The Southern University. I stayed on campus in the dorm rooms and had a taste of what the life of a college student at an HBCU was like. At that moment I chose Southern University and A&M college as the college I would be attending.

Although I was the first of my immediate family to graduate college, I had a lot of positive influences and mentors. All of which attended Southern University. Growing up in New Orleans in a low income, high crime neighborhood, college wasn't something that most of my peers focused on. I had been told by many that I was one of "the lucky ones." Being raised by a single mother who wasn't financially able to send me to college, I was often preached to about the importance of academics, extracurricular activities, and positive influences.

August 25, 2005 my family and I were faced with what we thought was the most horrific day of our lives when Hurricane Katrina hit New Orleans. I remember being a tenth grader and thinking our home, my friends, and everything else has been lost. Little did I know, in the midst of a storm, God was working everything out for my good. I relocated to Baton Rouge and attended Southern University Lab High School which was located on the campus of Southern University and A&M College. Being a part of the kitten's family truly helped me through my depression after Katrina. Not only did I meet lifelong friends I gained family. Being on the HBCU campus I was provided with resources needed to get through my high school years as normal as possible. I was provided clothes, assistance with my tuition, information on scholarships and pure love and support. The type of support that only an HBCU can provide. Once it was time for graduation and to apply for college, I only filled out one application and because of how dear it was to my heart, culture, and growth that application was of course to Southern University and A&M College. I just knew in my heart that there was no other college I wanted to attend and that I would get accepted. I prayed and one of the happiest days of my life was when I finally got my acceptance letter to enter the Fall 2008 Freshman class.

I could still remember the day I set up my dorm room at Shade Hall. My roommate and I were both so nervous to meet each other. We became best friends and scheduled all our classes together. It if wasn't for my roommate, suitemates, high school best friend, professors helping and being supportive, I would not have survived the struggles of a college student and earned my degree. Not only did I learn educational skills that made me the best candidate for a job but, being a student at an HBCU especially at Southern University taught me life skills and how to deal with any challenge that I would face in my career. I had professors that were more than just an educator. They were like second parents and mentors. They pushed me, they supported me, gave me advice, stayed on me about staying on my studies and pointed me in the right direction when it came to things like who and where to do internships to land a job. I learned skills such as utilizing your community and resources instead of just taking no for an answer.

I have so many great memories from my time at Southern University. One in particular is when the students rallied together and got many unregistered voters registered and played a major role in the election of the first black president of the United States, former

President Barack Obama. It was such an honor being a part of history. I can remember our classes were canceled to celebrate such a joyous occasion in black history. Professors, students, Campus Police, and other staff across campus and partied while singing "My President is Black" by rap artist young Jeezy. Things like this you just don't experience at a Predominantly White Institution. You have to be on an HBCU campus to understand and truly feel what that meant for black students and black people across the nation.

Another event that I would never forget while being on the campus of my HBCU is the tragic homicide of Travon Martin. Although Travon Martin was murdered in Florida, his murder felt very close to home. Like many college students all he was doing was walking with a hoodie on. This caused him to be racially profiled and murdered. I can remember how once again the students, staff and community around Southern University came together in peaceful protest and educational seminars on protecting yourself while being black. Again, these are things I feel as though I would have been able to experience at a Predominantly White Institution. Southern University even provided resources such as grief counseling for students in need after that event.

I truly enjoyed my time at my HBCU and remember the day I graduated from the Nelson Mandela College of Social Science with my Bachelor's degree in criminal justice. I was so grateful I cried tears of joy. Three months before graduation, I was sitting in the ICU fighting for my life after being diagnosed with a brain tumor and having emergency surgery. Before being discharged from the hospital doctors told me I needed to sit out the rest of the semester and try to finish the following year because "it would just be too hard for me to get from one side of campus to another and get caught up on my missed work". The next day I made contact with all of my professors who all agreed that I would walk across the stage as a Fall 2012 graduate. They vowed that they would do whatever it took to assist me. Once again, I repeat, "things like this you just don't experience at a Predominantly White Institution". Not only did I walk across the stage that December, by January 2013 I was enrolled in my Master's program at The Southern University and A&M college. Again, it was only one school on my list to apply to and that was SU.

Due to what I gained from Southern University I have been able to make a difference in youth in my community today. I assist with Justice reform in both juvenile and adult corrections, provide mental health service and resources to blacks throughout Louisiana, and have been a service to all mankind through my Sorority, Alpha Kappa Alpha Sorority Incorporated in the Nu Gamma Omega Chapter. My hope is that some little black girl who may not be from the best neighborhood, who may not grow up with both parents, who may not come from a family of college graduates, or may face many life challenges can know my story and know that she can still do it.

About Megan Daniels

Megan Daniels of New Orleans, La. Current resident of Baton Rouge, La. Is a Graduate of Southern University A&M College with a Bachelor and Masters of Science in Criminal Justice. Is he has been a member of Alpha Kappa Alpha Sorority inc. Nu Gamma Omega Chapter since Fall of 2017. Megan is the mother to her beautiful daughter Aris Lee Poullard and Second mom to nephew Nolan Taylor. Megan has been a part of many organizations providing resources and mental health services through her community.

Megan is currently serving on the Louisiana/Mississippi growth and Marketing team for Center Senior Primary Care as the Community Engagement Professional. She is owner and operator of Body to Sole Fitness in which she uses to provide resources on healthier ways of living through yoga, meditation, encouragement, and self-care. In her spare time, she enjoys time with family and pampering.

KENDALL BUNCH

Recruited For Greatness
Kendall Bunch

If I'm honest, I didn't know much about HBCUs before college. I knew most students were black, but my knowledge didn't extend further than that. I went to predominantly white grade schools and I applied to all predominantly white institutions (PWI). So, when I was approached about tennis recruitment for Southern University and A&M College, I said, "Where?"

However, the idea of attending an HBCU quickly became a desire. I went on two recruitment visits while being scouted for the schools' tennis teams. By the time I left each visit, I wanted to feel as though that university would give me the full college experience. At the time, that meant a balance of a great tennis program, a good fashion design program and a great social life. At the first school I visited, the women I met on the tennis team were great and very nice. However, by the end of my trip, I felt very underwhelmed by what the school had to offer.

On the flip side, after visiting Southern University, I was immediately sold. The women on the tennis team, who are now my forever teammates, showed me all aspects of college life. They were Southwestern Athletic Conference (SWAC) tennis champions, they took me to an Alpha Phi Alpha probate, we went shopping together and they showed me a glimpse of what college parties were like. Although Southern's fashion program didn't have everything the other university had to offer, Southern felt like "home". The following Fall '12 semester, I was moving my things into the freshman dorm, Samuella V. Totty Hall.

College did not disappoint. From the parties, to homecoming, to Bayou Classic, to continuing the SWAC championship streak with my tennis team and keeping up my grades in the classroom… I did it all! I built relationships with amazing people over the years, that I'm still friends with 'til this day.

Socially, you can never get bored at Southern. Whether you were going to the "Circle" to hang out as a freshman, going to Vibes 2.0 on a Friday night, heading to a kickback at the Palisades, attending a probate or going to Pretty Wednesday at The Union, there was always something to do. There were also groups and organizations that you can join on campus. There's Greek life, sports teams, student government, the band and dancers, etc. These groups created a social status integrated into HBCU culture. In my eyes, there were pros and cons associated with these groups. On one hand, it was easy to get caught up in status and appearance amongst your peers which can influence people to join these groups for the wrong reason. On the other end, you were building a network that can help you in your career and beyond. Blood couldn't make you any closer to your fellow group members. It also taught us how to market ourselves as professionals. To be part of these organizations, we must hold a certain amount of responsibility academically, in the community and socially, that crafts us into well-rounded individuals and sets us apart from Ivy League and PWI graduates who only focused on academics in school.

Being a student-athlete offered a unique, thrilling college experience for me. I formed priceless bonds with other athletes who understand the lifestyle of going to school and playing a sport. There was also a sense of pride that came from being a SWAC tennis champion three years in a row and bringing the wins back to my university. Even with the success we had as a team, every so often I would still run into students that would say, "We have a tennis team?" or "I never met a black girl that played tennis." It cracked me up every time. Nonetheless, respect for our athletic accomplishments carried throughout my collegiate career and there's no better feeling.

In the classroom, like many adolescents matriculating into higher education, I was still finding myself. I mentioned earlier that I wanted to major in fashion during college. Mid-way through my freshman year, I realized that wasn't for me. Sophomore year, I switched my major to communications with a concentration in public relations. That was the best decision I could've made, but I didn't know it at the time. I also had a passion for broadcast journalism. So, I explored all my options.

I completed a PR internship with the Media Relations department at Southern. I did another PR internship in Miami, FL the following summer. I hosted my own show on Southern's student-produced radio station. I interned with Max 94.1 with Kool DJ SupaMike and A.J. Boogie. I was part of Southern University's Geaux Team which promoted Southern's men's basketball team, hosted half-time shows, and increased crowd engagement.

I owe most of my knowledge in PR to my former professor Dr. Yolanda Campbell. I won multiple awards in her classes and she introduced me to the Public Relations Student Society of America (PRSSA). To this day, I am a member of the adult PRSA chapter. She equipped me with the resources and confidence I needed to enter "the real world". However, after graduating Cum Laude with my bachelor's degree, I could not find a job in PR for six months. I figured I'd switch things up and pursue my love for broadcast journalism.

I started my own entertainment media brand interviewing public figures like celebrity brand manager Karen Civil and actor Jackie Long. I attended New York Film Academy's broadcast journalism program. A year later I went back and earned my master's in journalism from Temple University in Philadelphia, PA. Upon graduating from Temple, I secured a TV news anchor and reporter job. I stayed at that job for two years before deciding to go back into PR. I now work as a publicist in Philadelphia making more than twice as much as I was making as a news anchor.

If it wasn't for all the internships I completed at Southern, I would not have the job I have today. As a result of attending Southern, I've met people from other HBCUs that have helped me advance in my career. I was at a journalism conference one year and met someone highly ranked at a TV station. He was not impressed with my resume at the time, if I'm honest. Even so, I distinctly remember him saying, "Because you went to an HBCU, I'm going to help you." That was in 2018 and to this day he has been one of the most influential people in my career and only a phone call away whenever I need career advice. Yes, you may have to wait in long lines in the Financial Aid office and some schools may not have as much money as a PWI but HBCUs produce greatness. You will leave having all the tools you need to succeed in life. I know I did!

About Kendall Bunch

Kendall Bunch, a publicist and life coach in Philadelphia, is one that believes there's no limits to what a woman can do. The New Jersey native moved to Florida with her parents at the age of 10, so she and her younger sister could pursue tennis year-round. That move paid off because she attended Southern University A&M College on a full athletic scholarship. That's when Kendall began exploring what the world had to offer her.

At Southern, Kendall hosted a student-led radio show, interned at MAX 94.1 with Kool DJ SupaMike and AJ Boogie and completed a PR internship in Miami, FL. She, also, handled business on the tennis court winning three SWAC championships with her tennis team. In 2016, the ambitious student-athlete graduated Cum Laude with a bachelor's degree in communications concentrated in Public Relations.

About six months post-grad, Kendall decided she wanted to be in front of the camera. For the next five years she chased after that desire, creating her own media brand "Kennii Live" interviewing celebrity brand manager Karen Civil and actor Jackie Long. She, also, attended a 4-week Journalism course at New York Film Academy. When she felt like that wasn't enough, Kendall continued her education at Temple University in Philadelphia, PA to earn her master's degree in journalism. She graduated with a news anchor and reporter job waiting for her in Michigan. There, she became an award-winning journalist. She, also, received her life coach certification to help women find their purpose.

Approaching the final six months of her contract at the news station, God told Kendall it was time for a shift in life. She decided to change careers. She headed back to the east coast and landed where she started, in public relations. Since then, she has not looked back. Kendall now thrives as a publicist for a major organization in Philadelphia with the goal to eventually open her own agency.

ALICIA SUTTON JONES

Sentenced to SUcceed, Failure Was Not an Option!
Alicia Sutton Jones

Historically black colleges and universities (HBCUs) have always been, and will always be, the cornerstone of black excellence. HBCUs serve as a village and cultivate a sense of belonging. I matriculated at Southern University as a young woman of color in that village but transitioned into a woman of value to my community. The Southern University System provided soil that was rich in nutrients of love, history, security, sisterhood, brotherhood, and solidarity.

Growing up in a single-parent household with a limited income in the Eden Park community of Baton Rouge was not easy, but my mother made it look like a piece of cake by not caving into any struggle, strain, or strife. No goals or tasks were unattainable in Yvonne's house. As such, I received multiple scholarships to attend out- of-state colleges to play volleyball and run track. However, I chose to stay home and attend Southern University to help support my mother and young brothers. Attending an HBCU in my hometown afforded me several opportunities and eliminated expensive out-of-state tuition and dormitory fees. I was awarded a Pell Grant that gave me the chance of a lifetime, and I didn't take it for granted. On the contrary, traveling this path made me work harder and ultimately fostered my passion to empower and encourage students from the Los Angeles area, as well as my native community, to attend the best HBCU on the planet. Serving in my current capacity as a 2-term Los Angeles Alumni Chapter President, I have the privilege of giving back to deserving, young students, and this passion is a direct result of the seeds that were planted in me during my Southern University college experience.

On April 21, 2023, I had a rare but awe-inspiring encounter that is indicative of the culture of an HBCU. I was attending an event in Baton Rouge and was approached by one of my college professors, Dr. Rosalind Reynard. She said, "Do you remember me, Alicia?" Recognizing her immediately, I replied, "Yes ma'am, Dr. Reynard, I know who you are." The conversation progressed to this jaw-dropping, explosive moment. "Alicia, I will never forget your presentation in my psychology class. It was so impactful that everyone in the class was crying." I was shocked as I looked at her with tears in my eyes. I had not seen my professor since I left Southern University in 1994, over 29 years ago! I was both stunned and emotional that she remembered the young girl from 38th Street in Eden Park. Dr. Reynard was instrumental in my decision to change my major from nursing to psychology. This speaks to the phenomenal impact of HBCUs where you are not just a number; you are somebody!

Southern University embodies a culture of support for students, not only academically but also personally. I was blessed to have many professors and administrators that were there for me, whatever the challenge. I had specific people that I could go to at any time who emphasized that there was an open-door policy whenever I needed assistance. I never felt like I was navigating those challenges alone. This support system allowed me to flourish and soar so that I could focus on the things that were within my power, like obtaining a quality education.

Having an HBCU like Southern to support my educational aspirations was crucial. Whenever I encountered any type of issue with my classes, Mrs. LaJoyce Wilson, Junior Division Advisor, answered the call to guide me. If there was a problem with my Pell Grant paperwork, the late Mr. James "Billy" Cannon in the Budget/Comptroller's office was intentional about assisting me in getting it resolved. I didn't ever have to worry! Mr. Cannon also recommended me for work study to provide administrative support at the Physical Plant, now known as Facility Services, under the supervision of Ms. Athel Martin. Ms. Martin gave me the opportunity to study hard and learn the ins and outs of all the buildings and keys to every door on the campus. Working in the plant was like having an internship. It enhanced my clerical, writing, people, and leadership skills, and was a great addition to my resume upon graduating. I was blessed to work at the Physical Plant during my entire college career and culminated that experience with lots of knowledge and opportunities that were integral for my success.

One couldn't attend Southern University without having a great time, making memories and friends that would last a lifetime. I had so many opportunities to obtain a sense of community, like vying for Miss Freshman; although I didn't win, it was an incredible experience that I will never forget. I loved to sing and was invited by one of my college friends, Sherri Moses, to join the gospel singing group "Women with a Vision." Women, as we were eloquently called, sang all over the campus for different events. One occasion, we received notice from the late Dr. Isaac Greggs that he wanted Women to do some background singing with our world-renowned band, the Human Jukebox. Who knew this would foster a relationship with the band, traveling on bus number four with the Fabulous Dancing Dolls and singing during the Battle of the Bands as well as half- time shows for the Bayou Classic? We would receive $10 stipends and a trip to Piccadilly Cafeteria in Delmont Village either before or after we performed. We didn't have to change who we were because of our beliefs and faith in God. We didn't have to be ashamed about giving God praise publicly at school. Dr. Greggs embraced it and supported us and our vision of being young women on the campus who were sold out for Christ. Although we were "Women with a Vision", three members of this powerful gospel group could not have fathomed that our paths would eventually lead to becoming Southern University Alumni Federation Chapter Presidents (Erica Moses and I), and LaQuitta Thomas becoming the first female National SUAF President in the history of the university.

Post Southern University, I have had some remarkable experiences both personally and professionally. As a published author, advocate, and entrepreneur, I am grateful for humble beginnings and collegiate opportunities that helped set me up for success. I have been married for 32 years to my wonderful husband, Greg, who also attended THE Southern University. I am the proud mother of my beautiful special needs daughter, Genesis, who is the apple of my eye and my WHY for serving on the board of directors for, Special Needs Network, one of the most prestigious special needs organizations in the state of California. I have made it my life's work to give back and encourage others as I, too, am a beneficiary of the rich deposits that were invested in me. For whom much is given, much is required. I am not only a product of the HBCU experience; I am Southern! Excellence defines us, pride sustains us, and tradition guides us.

About Alicia Sutton Jones

Alicia Sutton Jones is a motivational speaker, entrepreneur, grief coach, mentor, and author of Sentenced to Live. She earned a Bachelor of Science in Psychology at Southern University and A&M College and received her grief coach certification with the Institution of Professional Grief Coaching in Washington, DC. She served in management roles in the mortgage industry for 15 years where she assisted families impacted by Hurricane Katrina.

Alicia is the Chief Operating Officer and Director of Events for Smokey Note Entertainment and Owner/Managing Partner of Affluence Executive Transport. Current President of Southern University Alumni Los Angeles Chapter, Alicia is a Life Member of the Southern University Alumni Federation and serves on the SUAF National Executive Council. She is a member of the Special Needs Network Board of Directors and an avid volunteer for Forever Footprints, which provides support for families suffering from pregnancy or infant loss. Alicia is the wife of Greg and proud parent of her special needs daughter, Gen.

BRITTANY PRICE

Good Things Come to the Determined,
An Accomplished Journey
Brittany Price

Determination. This is what I was faced with in every step of my tenure at Southern University. The meaning of determined is to firmly be set in one's decision or course of action, especially with the aim of achieving a particular goal (*dictionary.com*). Southern has taught me that good things come to those who are determined to go get it.

Truth be told, I barely made it in as a student at Southern University when I applied. As a high school student, I took so many ACT and SAT tests in hope to increase my scores each time. On my last ACT test, I finally made the required score to get in. However, that came with having to take a Compass test over the summer to be considered conditionally approved. This is when that determination gene kicked in. Southern University was the first and only school I applied to. I had no choice but to get in if I had any shot of being a college student. It was Compass test day, and I was more than ready to become a Jaguar after weeks of studying. I took the test and awaited the results. Weeks later, in the form of a physical letter, my results read, "Congratulations, you have been Conditionally Approved!" I was becoming a first-generation college student.

As an incoming freshman, I knew I had to set the bar high to prove to my friends, my family, and myself that I could survive college on my own. On the other hand, I didn't know where to begin. In 2009, Southern taught me what it really meant to have that Jaguar Spirit. I attended all campus activities, pageants, sport games and started joining campus clubs to be more involved. I was making a smooth transition from a high school student to a Southernite. Since I was a dancer in high school, I wanted to audition for a spot on the Southern University's dance teams. Unfortunately, I never became a member of any of the teams, but I knew dance was my passion. I continued to train in dance outside of college and was determined to follow my dreams of being a professional dancer one day. I carried that determination throughout my Sophomore and Junior year. I knew I wanted to be a part of something bigger than myself. Fall 2011, I was honored to achieve one of the happiest moments of my life, I became a member of Alpha Kappa Alpha Sorority, Incorporated. I was able to serve my community as the chapter's Ivy Leaf Reporter as well as showcase my abilities in dance and stepping as the step master at the Greek shows. I love every moment of my undergraduate experience as a member of the Beta Psi Chapter. That same year, I became an orientation leader for what is now called Jaguar 360, mentoring the next set of incoming freshman students entering Southern. This is the year I was molded into the woman I am today.

In 2013, I was a graduating senior reflecting on all my accomplishments I achieved in school. I received the Chancellor's Award, was crowned homecoming dorm queen twice, consistently made the Dean's List, was involved in several college clubs, became a member of a sorority, and was now receiving my Bachelor's of Arts degree in Mass Communication. I started interning at a local news station and was determined to be hired for a position in my field of study. After months interning, I was offered a position as a tv production editor. In 2014, I decided to attend Graduate school to major in Public Administration and became the graduate assistant to the Dean of Students where I was a mentor to the undergraduate students. I felt this was a way to give myself a second shot at doing college the way I intended, with experience. I was content with my life, but I wanted more. That determination gene activated once more. In my first graduate year, I was granted the opportunity by Career Services, under the direction of Mrs. Tamara Montgomery and Mr. Eric Pugh, to represent Southern as a student participant for the Thurgood Marshall College Fund career fair. I represented Southern University in front of hundreds of HBCU participants and 60 Fortune 500 companies. By the end of the career fair, I was given several employment offers by these fortune 500 companies. One in which I accepted and started my career in sales.

At the Thurgood Marshall College Fund Career Fair in 2017, I was granted the opportunity to represent Southern University again, this time as a participant and an employee of a fortune 500 company. This visit felt special since I was doing this with my younger sister, who was a freshman at the time. I made sure that I was giving her my personal blueprint on how to succeed and thrive at Southern upon leaving.

That May, I graduated and received my Master's degree in Public Administration and started working as a sales professional. This has provided me with years of sales experience and the opportunity to live in different states of the country. I have been able to utilize my degrees with recruiting and being a part of the creation of two companies' official marketing videos. Simultaneously, I went on to become a professional dancer for an Arena Football League, an East Coast Hockey League, the Women's National Basketball Association, and the National Football League. I've had the privilege to perform in front of thousands of fans with major artists such as Kanye West, Teddy Riley, Tamar Braxton, and Keith Sweat. Southern University has afforded me with long lasting friendships with my peers and former professors who have been in my corner since I entered the University in 2009. I would like to give special thanks to professors, Mr. Darrell Roberson and Dr. Fuller for introducing my love for communications and media and Dr. Rufus Nwogu for making my graduate school experience positively fulfilling. My advice to any student at Southern is to make college what you would like it to be. Don't be afraid to take chances, stay determined to achieve your goals and be okay with doing college at your own pace. Lastly, take advantage of all opportunities and resources it is providing to ensure you are graduating feeling successful and accomplished.

About Brittany Price

Brittany Price is a native of Lake Charles, LA currently residing in Atlanta, GA. She is a two-time graduate from Southern University A&M College holding a Bachelors of Art degree in Mass Communication and a Masters of Public Policy in Public Administration. She is also a member of Alpha Kappa Alpha Sorority, Inc. Currently, she is a professional actress and dancer that has performed with artist such as lil Yatchy, Kanye West, Keith Sweat, Guy, and Teddy Riley.

SAGE EDGERSON

Jag for Life

Sage Edgerson

Growing up, one of my favorite tv shows was *A Different World*. It gave me a lens of what life at an HBCU would be like. Because I have always known I would always attend a Historically Black College, I dreamed of the café, the parties, the classes, and the students I'd encounter. My late mom, Susan Edgerson, an attendee of Southern University and A&M College in the 70s, graduate and former adjunct professor, and Title IV-E Child Welfare Program Director at the School of Social Work at Southern University in New Orleans, always promoted black excellence and advancement of our people through social work, education, and activism. What better way to continue those ideas instilled in her child than sending her to Southern University and A&M College?

The choice of what HBCU to attend wasn't mine, but I wouldn't want it to be any other way. I'm grateful for that decision. My destiny would be at Southern University and A&M College in the fall of 2010, where my true journey began. Green, like most first-year students, I instantly thought once I was on the yard, my mom was gone, and I was set up in Totty Hall, my black college experience I dreamed about would start. However, it didn't start immediately; it took time. Though discouraged that it wasn't what I expected at first, the fuel to stick it out and prosper was the black college experience. I had to be patient because it was true what some people say; you must wait for what is genuinely for you.

Once I fully understood that the experience was all my own and didn't always look like *A Different World* or like my peers, I began to bloom. I authentically paved the way for myself and curated my life on campus, something I advocate all people should do. First, it started with finding my tribe. Who were my people on campus? A misconception about HBCUs is that they aren't as inclusive as other universities, but that is far from the truth. Yes, black people make up the majority of people on campus, but you get to know the varying cultures within the different groups of black people. Where they are from, and what their life looked like. We're rewarded with being able to understand all walks of black people. Black people from different parts of the country and also people from all over the world. HBCUs aren't just for black people because higher learning is for everyone. What HBCUs represent is for everyone to celebrate. Something I appreciated the most was the true diversity of HBCU culture.

I planted the seeds of my HBCU experience during my first few semesters. Once I found my tribe or The Crew, my shell started to crack. I began to navigate and balance my social life and schooling life. I became involved on campus, switched majors, and appreciated every stepping stone each semester. SU was where I decided it was ok to indulge in my creative passions and be realistic about them. I honed in on my love for fashion and became a student of fashion in Pinkie Thrift Hall. I walked in all the fashion shows on campus until I graduated and even made connections in the film industry. On the yard, I discovered that my deep love of music could be a career, and I began to DJ, thanks to The Crew. Not only did I DJ, but I also had a hand in resurrecting the Yards radio station and being music manager for a short period. I began my journey in activism by becoming VP of the NAACP chapter and started to lay the foundation to bridge the gap between SU's and LSU's black students. I even wore a crown as SU's first Miss Natural Hair and the natural hair club president. I attended house parties, kickbacks, pageants, and campus events. I hung out in the circle and at the union. I made every red beans & rice Monday and fried fish Friday, and I'd also swipe my off-campus friends in. I did life and student life, and what Southern University taught me was something intangible about life and adulthood that I carry daily. To be your own person, curate and cultivate your life, and the famous tagline we Southernites know and echo, "If you can make it at SU, you can make it anywhere!" That was my black college experience. If I can make it here, I could make it anywhere. Unapologetically and audaciously, I'd make it anywhere because my HBCU prepared me, and I took heed to all the themes presented. I had complete control of my destiny. SU gave me a journal, and I wrote the script.

Through time, lessons, and battles, I found my ever-growing voice, ambitions, creativity, passions, and my tribe, and it would not have been without my choice to continue a legacy of black education and excellence that my mom paved the way for, that those before her did as well. Those things have shaped the woman I am today and the woman into which I'm continuing to evolve. My HBCU nurtured me and gave me pride. I've always been an, "I'm Black, and I'm proud!" person. Still, to know I continued on a dream and the ambitions of our founding fathers, pride isn't a big enough word to honestly describe my experience and elation to say I am a graduate of a Historically Black College and University, but also to say my HBCU is the oldest HBCU college system with five campuses and hopefully counting. I'd do all five years over again, not for a re-do to change but because those were the best years of my life. They were transformative, chaotic, hilarious, and challenging because I made it all my own, on my own terms, and my HBCU was the incubator as it was for my mom, myself, friends, and future generations. I've made lifelong friends, robust connections, and truly iconic memories. That's my HBCU experience at THEE Southern University and A&M College, defender always of the Columbia blue and gold, a proud Jag for life.

About Sage Edgerson

Sage Edgerson or Legatron Prime is a New Orleans native, multi-genre DJ, Producer, Film & TV Costumer, Wardrobe Stylist, Creative Director, and Vibe curator.

She is 1/3 of New Orleans' only monthly for women, by women party, Where My Girls At? NOLA, Saturday night headliner at The Dragons Den with her weekly jam, PRIMETIME since 2017, along with a host of venues, festivals and events including Hi Ho Lounge, BUKU Festival, Essence Festival and Boiler Room/Freewater under her belt since getting her professional start in 2015. For any party she rocks, she makes it known that it's a "CONSENT ONLY DANCE FLOOR!".

She emphasizes cultural influence and preservation in the city of New Orleans while working with her colleagues, local brands, and artists to push the music and creative scene forward.

ERIN D. ROGERS, MPH&TM, MS

"The Power of the KREWE"
Erin D. Rogers, MPH&TM, MS

The clock struck midnight – Monday morning hysteria filled the air as anxious students vying for leadership positions hastened to secure their campaign headquarters—the hub of excitement for student elections. The intensity of that moment left me jolted until my sorority sister looked me in my face, shook me slightly, and forcefully said – ERIN, it's your time; let's go! This began the exciting journey of me becoming the 82nd Miss Southern University A&M College.

Campaign Week at Southern University was like nothing I have ever experienced. I truly felt like I was running in a statewide political campaign. As I reflect on that time, I am left wondering how I balanced everything. The days were so long with campaigning between classes, balancing my rigorous Pre-Med schedule, and dorm raiding at night. Moreover, I have to give credit to my team, campaign manager (Erin Smith), family, and friends who held me up during this process: from making sure I was taking care of myself physically, to helping me move my entire apartment during campaign week (thanks, Sekoya, Marissa, and Jasmine), and even running my social media pages (thanks, Kinda @thatkindaluv). It took a herculean effort to push through that week.

Thus, having a solid theme was the cornerstone of a successful campaign at Southern University. I credit my brilliant sister (Erica Rogers) with curating my theme; we adapted the fanfare of Mardi Gras and merged other elements of Louisiana culture. It was so fitting, and slightly advantageous, with me being a Louisiana native. Everything was perfectly crafted, from my slogan, "Join Erin's KREWE for Miss SU," to the carnival-colored T-shirts, the customized Mardi Gras beads, second-line umbrellas hand crafted by my mother, the New Orleans Indians, the enormous billboards and yard signs that flooded every inch of campus, and, not to mention, a parade float.

The excitement grew as the week continued; Pretty Wednesday was considered the most important campaign day next to Election Day. This was the day that you needed to make a lasting impression, and that we did! We had a traditional New Orleans second-line with the Mardi Gras Indians. The Indians' costumes alone made a lasting statement with the intricate details and the vibrantly colored feathers. The performance was more than just a campaign strategy; it was an immersive experience and expression of black Louisiana culture. What made this moment even more memorable was that the candidate for SGA President (Willie McCorkle) gathered a few of his friends and created a second-line band. Although Willie's second-line band was not planned, it foreshadowed our teams merging to become SGA President and Miss Southern University.

The Queen's Revue was another defining moment in the journey of becoming Miss Southern University. This was an opportunity in showcasing your beauty, talent, and intellect. I was able to articulate my platform and plans to the student body which was very well received and executed. The time came, and I had to face my fear of showcasing myself in a swimsuit for the entire student body, talk about nerve-racking. In keeping with the theme, I had a carnival queen mantle created with tall white ostrich feathers in addition to "VOTE ERIN" in Swarovski crystal. I felt so confident in that moment, and I owned the stage like I was a Victoria's Secret model.

ELECTION DAY finally arrived, and all roads led to the polls. The day began on such a high note. For the first time in election history, a candidate had a Mardi Gras float on campus. We flooded the campus with Mardi Gras throws, push cards, and other campaign materials. If Instagram and TikTok had been around, it would have been a viral moment. As the day progressed, my body went into fight or flight mode, and I was hyper-focused on ensuring I got as many students to the polls. My determination pushed me further, and I did a last-minute dorm raid and drove students to the polls. That last push got me 75 additional votes.

It was finally 5:00 pm, and the polls were closed. People rushed to the Student Union to hear the results; I had other plans. If you could believe it, I am extremely introverted, and my social battery was so drained. I needed a moment to collect myself; not to mention my phone died, and no one could get ahold of me. I decided to sit by the lake near Mayberry Cafeteria to breathe and reflect on the past week. I can't lie; I was scared to hear the results. However, God sent me confirmation through a beautiful person named Bradley. He sat with me as I was contemplating walking to the Union. He said plainly, "Erin, you WON; you put in the hard work. Don't miss your moment!" His spirit calmed me, and after that exchange, I built up the courage to take that walk to the Union to face my fate. Unfortunately, I never got a chance to thank him and let him know how his affirming words significantly impacted me. Therefore, at this moment, I want to thank you, Bradley, from the bottom of my heart, and may your beautiful soul rest in peace.

From the moment I walked into the Union, I was ecstatically greeted by the "KREWE," family, friends, sorority sisters, and other student leaders; at that moment, I knew my life had completely changed, and that I would be etched into the Southern University history books. I cannot express the feeling I had but with utter joy, and, just like that, my reign had officially begun. As I was trying to wrap my mind around what just happened, the planning for the upcoming football season started. I was being pulled in many different directions and having to make decisions regarding the coronation, style of crowns, sashes, and attire for the Royal Court. I had to consider a lot so soon; however, I wouldn't have traded that moment for anything.

Lastly, I would not have been able to achieve such a high honor without the love and support of my family, friends and, most importantly, the KREWE. I am eternally grateful. To my Royal Court and Court Advisors, I will forever cherish the memories we shared and your influence on my life; it will forever live within my heart.

With Love,

Erin D. Rogers, MPH&TM, MS
82nd Miss Southern University A&M College

About Erin D. Rogers, MPH&TM, MS

Erin Dominique Rogers is a native of Laplace, Louisiana. Erin began her undergraduate career at Southern University and A&M College in the fall of 2009. Her exceptional character, commitment, leadership, perseverance, and dedication have been remarkable throughout her college and graduate career. She was a Fall 2011 initiate of the Beta Psi Chapter of Alpha Kappa Alpha Sorority, Incorporated. She was also active during her matriculation at Southern University; she was elected Miss Freshman 2009-2010, a member of Collegiate 100 Black Women, and Miss Southern University 2012-2013, among many other honors.

Erin graduated from Southern University A&M College in the Fall of 2013 and continued to obtain a Master of Public Health & Tropical Medicine (MPH&TM) from Tulane School of Public Health & Tropical Medicine and a Masters of Medical Science at Mississippi College. Following graduation, Erin became the Public Health Director for Braveheart Foundation, a non-profit humanitarian aid organization where they travel to remote villages in Uganda, Africa providing acute medical care and sustainable programs. She also serves as a Public Health Practicum Advisor providing mentorship and guidance to future Public Health Practitioners.

In August 2021, Erin joined the fight against COVID-19 Pandemic as a CDC Foundation Fellow; she has collaborated with the Louisiana Department of Health COVID-19 Testing Taskforce to ensure the equitable distribution of COVID-19 Testing Supplies statewide. During her time with the CDC Foundation, she has played a vital role in the development and execution of COVID-19 testing programs for Louisianans. Among her accomplishments, she has raised awareness of the Safer, Smarter Schools program, implemented an automated system for processing Testing Requests, was a part of the strategic planning during the Omicron Surge, and led the design of an Internal and Public-facing COVID-19 Testing Dashboard. She believes all her life experiences have been necessary to bring her to this juncture.

BRITTANY N. CRETCHAIN, MPA

Great Adventures on the Bluff
Brittany N. Cretchain, MPA

My HBCU experience at Southern University and A&M college was life changing. As a child, my mom would take my sister and I to most of Southern University's football and basketball games, homecoming Greek shows, Bayou Classic, probates, and other campus events, so I knew someday I would be a proud graduate of Southern University and A&M College. I am a native of Opelousas, Louisiana and the daughter of Susan and David Cretchain. Opelousas is home to many Southern University graduates. I was one of the many of my family members who graduated from Southern University. I received my Bachelor of Arts degree from Southern University and A&M College on December 14, 2012, and I obtained my Master of Science degree in Public Administration from Southern University and A&M College on December 10, 2021. One of my favorite quotes about Southern University is, "My parents raised me, but SU made me." SU truly helped mold me into the person I am today.

I knew that choosing a Historically Black College and University (HBCU) would not only allow me to learn more about my culture, but it would also surround me with other individuals who looked like me. I'll never forget in the fall of 2009 when I had History 115 with Dr. Charles Vincent. One day, he walked into the classroom and told us to close our books. Dr. Vincent said, "Your books are not needed because your history lesson for today is sitting right here in this classroom." Dr. Vincent called Mychal Bell to the front of the classroom to tell his story about the 'Jena Six.' Mychal Bell and five other black teens made national headlines in 2006. I was thrilled to hear the story first-hand, and, as a class, we learned Mychal's side of the story, which is a story I'll never forget. As Bell concluded his story to the class, Dr. Vincent told us, "Class, that's history, and one day, when your children or grandchildren are in school, or maybe sitting where you are, they will be reading about the 'Jena Six' in their history books.

Throughout my collegiate career, I connected with many people from all over the world who have become friends. During my undergraduate tenure at Southern University, I met some friends who became family, and I have so many great memories that will remain in my heart for a lifetime. When speaking about my beloved alma mater, I always tell people that my undergraduate experience was the best four years of my life, and no amount of money could ever pay for the education and experience I received at Southern University. Every time I cross "The hump," I get this overwhelming sense of pride, and I always say "I'm home." Southern University has served as my haven, a place where I can be unapologetically Black. The discussions that take place in our classrooms go beyond the four walls of our illustrious institutions. Instead, we take those life lessons and skills with us and apply them to our daily lives.

Moreover, attending Southern University took me out of my comfort zone and helped me live up to my full potential. Luckily, with the help of my professors and mentors, this shy, small-town girl was able to grow professionally and as a person overall. Attending Southern University and A&M College was one of the best decisions I've ever made, and I will forever be grateful for the knowledge my beloved alma mater has instilled in me. Coursework under my belt, I entered the Department of Mass Communication. Great professors such as Dr. Lorraine Fuller, Mr. Darrell Roberson, and Mr. Michael Cabel played pivotal roles in my academic achievements and helped me sharpen my broadcasting skills. I spent plenty of long hours in Stewart Hall, but all those long hours and challenges I faced prepared me for many different roles when I landed jobs at KATC-TV station (ABC affiliate) and KLAF/KADN (NBC and Fox affiliate) both located in Lafayette, Louisiana. Also, the skills that were instilled in me at home transitioned with me to college because my mom never allowed me to miss school; therefore, in college, I never missed class even on rainy days. Rainy days equals extra points.

At the age of eighteen, I moved onto campus where I resided in Camille Shade Hall. I enjoyed living there because it faces "the circle" where everyone would often gather after class and on the weekends. Living in the dormitory was my first introduction to independent living without parental supervision. It was a little shocking living on my own, but campus life felt like a safe community. All my life I had my own room, so sharing a room with a stranger can be challenging for some people; however, for me, I was blessed with one of the best roommates, Kayla Smith. We got along really well and respected each other's space. We're still friends and sorority sisters. At SU, if you lived in a dorm, a meal plan was required. One of the best parts about an HBCU experience is the dining halls. We lived for red beans and fried chicken on Mondays and fried fish Fridays. It was normal to have pep rallies and other festivities around campus. You could be walking back to your dorm and notice, out of nowhere, a full-blown party has formed in the circle. There would be students gathering, Greeks strolling, and a DJ blasting music in broad daylight. I didn't ask questions, I just went. Later, during my collegiate career, I learned, if possible, not to schedule any noon classes on Monday, Wednesday and Fridays. At SU we called Wednesday "Pretty Wednesday" which is when everyone would dress up for class and meet at the union at noon. Sometimes, depending on what was going on, there was a DJ present at the student union on Pretty Wednesdays. We've all lived that on-campus life and appreciated the value it added to our HBCU experience.

Being an alumna of Southern University and A&M College, I now have an extended family. Friendships, parties, the all-night study sessions become cherished memories for a lifetime. Your professors know where you are and what it takes to get you where you want to be. My school pride will always be with me, and nothing will change that. Growth is inevitable. At SU, I discovered more about myself than ever before. I was challenged culturally, intellectually, politically, and professionally. I'm forever grateful to be a two-time graduate of Southern University and A&M College. O Southern, Dear Southern, we owe our all to thee.

About Brittany N. Cretchain, MPA

Brittany was born and raised in Opelousas, Louisiana where she attended South Street Elementary, East Junior High and Opelousas Senior High School where she graduated in 2008. She received her Bachelor's of Arts Degree in Mass Communication with a concentration in Broadcasting from Southern University and A&M College in the Fall of 2012. While in undergraduate at Southern University and A&M College Brittany was on the Dean's list, an active member of the National Association of Black Journalists (NABJ), and a spring 2012 inductee of Collegiate 100 Black Women of SU. While working from home during the global pandemic in August 2020 Brittany enrolled into the Executive Master of Science in Public Administration online (EMPA) program at Southern University and A&M College. She graduated with her master's in public administration in the Fall of 2021 (school so nice she went back twice).

Currently, Brittany is an Economic Development Specialist for St. Landry Parish Economic Development. Brittany supports the mission and values of St. Landry Economic Development (the "organization" or "SLED") by operating as a strategic "right hand" to the Chief Executive Officer (CEO). Brittany's role primary focus is on business retention and industrial job opportunities by attracting new and retaining existing commercial and industrial business opportunities throughout St. Landry Parish, Louisiana. Also, in this role Brittany proactively engages in networking and business development events with owners, developers, and stakeholders to help navigate issues, develop connections and maintain relationships.

In her free time, Brittany loves volunteering in her community, spending time with family and friends, cheering on her SU Jags, working out and reading. She continues to give back to her beloved alma mater by being a football season ticket holder, a member of SU Alumni Federation and the Southern University Quarterback club. Also, Brittany is a proud and active member of Alpha Kappa Alpha Sorority, Incorporated-Lambda Beta Omega Chapter and Junior League of Lafayette.

SHARLENE PRYER

An Athlete's Dream
Sharlene Pryer

The culture at Southern University is not only rooted in African and African American culture but also focused on student achievement. Many of my family members are proud graduates of HBCUs. Learning about the rich history of the institution and the long list of notable alumni, I knew that I would not have the same opportunities if I did not attend a HBCU, specifically Southern University. As a child from Morgan City, LA I grew up attending the Bayou Classic as well as football and basketball games for years with my family. My mother graduated from Southern University in 1973 and my sister graduated in 2006. Also, my cousin, Herman Hartman, coached the Women's Basketball team at Southern University from 1992 to 2000. With many of my other family members being SUBR alumni or former faculty members, I have always loved the familial culture of SU and it always felt like home, even as a child.

I always had dreams of playing collegiate volleyball or softball. During my senior year of high school, I was recruited to play volleyball at Southern University, Mississippi Valley State University, and the University of Arkansas at Pine Bluff and softball at Louisiana College. During one of my high school volleyball games, Southern's Head Volleyball Coach, Nathaniel Denu was in attendance. After the game, he spoke to me, and my mother and I was offered a four-year scholarship to play volleyball at Southern University. He assured my mother that I would be well taken care of and that getting an education was the top priority. Being that the majority of my schooling and athletic career had been around predominantly white individuals, I was not only excited for this opportunity, but I was ready for a change. Having the opportunity to play volleyball at a collegiate level and at a university with familial ties was truly an honor. I knew attending Southern University A&M College was the right choice.

In August of 2007, my mother and aunt helped move my things into Shade Hall. I was nervous, but I was also excited to begin my journey at Southern University as a student-athlete. I had to be on campus early to prepare for pre-season training and to meet my new teammates. Pre-season was brutal and tested my mental toughness. My teammates informed all the freshmen of the trainer named ZEUS. No matter what they told us, it did not prepare any of us freshmen for what was to come. On my first day of training, we were to be at the track at 5:00 a.m. to begin training at 5:30 a.m. I vividly remember not knowing what to expect. Zeus' SUV pulled up to the track, he stepped out of his SUV and yelled "TAKE OFF." The warm up felt like a workout and all I could think was, "I have to come back and do this tomorrow?" I think that day we ran a minimum of 6 miles. That was only the first workout of our long two weeks of 2-a days. Zeus certainly taught me perseverance, because I had no choice, but to keep going no matter how tired I was. The reality of being a student-athlete is that you will dedicate countless hours to training, practicing, and traveling, while keeping up with classwork. Coach Denu made sure we were dedicated to our studies and attended study hall regularly. He made sure we knew our main goal was to leave Southern University with a degree. Being that busy all of the time and having so much to accomplish in a finite number of hours, I perfected the art of multitasking. I learned to juggle more tasks than I thought was possible, and I learned how to devote enough attention to each one to avoid letting any areas suffer. However, one of the best gifts that athletics gave me is the relationships and friendships that I formed along the way.

In the Fall of 2009, I was initiated into the Beta Psi Chapter of Alpha Kappa Alpha Chapter, Incorporated. Becoming a member of such an illustrious sorority was a dream come true. There were several inspirational women in my life that were AKAs and so I never really considered joining any other organization. Joining the sisterhood of Black women has brought me friendships beyond the campus and my undergraduate years.

As a speech pathology major, seeing Speech-Language Pathologists of color was so inspiring. According to the American Speech-Language-Hearing Association, only eight percent of its members identify as a racial minority. Knowing that there is such a disparity of people of color in the particular field, I was enlightened to see people like me with such knowledge and insight. I was so motivated by the wisdom from my professors and the support I received; I immediately went on to obtain my Masters of Speech Pathology at Southern University. My experience in the program led me to pursue more and learn more about the gap in representation. I am currently pursuing a Doctorate in speech pathology because of the profound impact left by my professors and mentors.

My experience as a student-athlete and becoming a member of Alpha Kappa Alpha Sorority, Incorporated brought me so much joy while also teaching me what I can accomplish is limitless. I also met my husband Belfred Jr. aka "TJ" on the campus of Southern University. I will especially forever be indebted for my time at SU, it is because of an HBCU that we met and started our great journey together.

While there are many worthy aspects of an education at an HBCU, I feel the most exclusive aspect of the SU experience is its supportive environment. My years at Southern University were beyond what I could have imagined. Attending and graduating from SU has afforded me a plethora of opportunities and lifelong friends. Being black and graduating with people who not only looked like me but shared comparable ambitions of the world is a beautiful thing. Attending SU furthermore helped me discover so much about myself as a black woman while challenging me to step outside of my comfort zone in various ways. I will forever be grateful for such an experience over the years at Southern University. #ForeverSU

About Sharlene Pryer

Sharlene is a 2011 graduate of Southern University A&M College. While at Southern University A&M College, Sharlene was member of the Woman's Volleyball team, and she is also a member of the Alpha Kappa Alpha Sorority Incorporated. Upon graduation, Sharlene furthered her education at Southern University by obtaining a master's degree in 2013. Sharlene currently works as a certified Speech Language Pathologist where she is licensed in Louisiana, Texas and California and she is presently working towards her doctoral degree in Speech Pathology.

BELFRED "TJ" PRYER, JR.

A Vision Turned Reality
Belfred "TJ" Pryer, Jr.

I graduated from Southern University A&M college in May of 2011 with my Bachelors in Business with a concentration in Entrepreneurship. I was born and raised in Maringouin, Louisiana, which is roughly thirty miles from Southern University. Being that my mom is from New Orleans, our family would frequent the Bayou Classic, and many of my family members would tailgate during the football season. Those were my earliest memories of being in the SU atmosphere.

As a child, my dreams were to become a professional athlete. I grew up watching my father and uncle play baseball in the "Sugar Cane League" on the weekends. My childhood was filled with sporting events, and I thrived on competition even as a young kid. In high school, I had offers to play football and baseball at various colleges and committed to Belhaven College in my last year of high school. I received a phone call from Roger Cador in the summer of 2006. My dad answered, and, after a few minutes on the phone with Coach Cador, I was on my way to Southern University in the fall of 2006 to play baseball. My older cousins, Melvin Anderson and Mike Woods, who went on to play professionally in the Major League both played baseball at Southern under the leadership of Coach Roger Cador. Therefore, being able to follow in their footsteps was a vision that became a reality to continue a family tradition.

I vividly remember my first days on campus. My parents moved me into an "old" Jones dormitory. We did know we were in the wrong dorm, and I soon moved to "new" Jones which is located in the back of campus along with the baseball players. Our first day of baseball practice was an early one. Morning practices started before the sun came up. Unfortunately, my roommate and I were late getting to the practice. Getting from the back of campus to the front without a car can be a challenge. When we finally made it to the front of campus, we noticed some people were running. It was not unusual to see other players running, because many of the fall sporting programs were preparing for their respective seasons. We quickly jumped in line and began running; therefore, Coach would not realize we were late. Something seemed off as we were running, and I asked one of the players, "What position do you play?", they responded, "we run track." Unbeknownst to us, my roommate and I were at the wrong spot with the wrong team. We quickly ran to the baseball field, and it was no secret that we were beyond late. Despite that mishap, we became like brothers on the baseball team. In 2009, we won the Southwestern Athletic Conference Championship. That truly is the goal we set out to achieve as brothers each season. Coach Cador's legacy runs deep and to have a championship while under his leadership was a dream. During my senior year of playing baseball, it was bittersweet knowing my time of playing collegiate ball was coming to an end. I definitely learned more than the game of baseball. Coach Cador had strict rules that I did not always understand, but they were put in place to make us not only better players, but better men.

As for combining schoolwork and playing baseball, it was not an easy task at first. When I initially got to campus, my main focus was baseball. I discovered a network of professors and informal mentors who made sure I was prepared beyond baseball. While I spent most of my time in T.T. Allain, I had many professors that supported me throughout my years. Mr. Marcel instilled resilience and Dr. Clark made sure that education was prioritized along with athletic obligations. Ms. M. Hughes took great care of me ensuring I was on the path to graduate. My professors provided a challenging, educational atmosphere with a solid foundation. It was a familiarity with everyone that made understanding and learning personal. I really appreciate the genuine investment professors felt toward my success. I was supported by all my professors, and they did everything possible to make sure I had the skills to be productive post-graduation.

My experience at SUBR was full of memories and opportunities I know I could not experience anywhere else. From Wednesdays in the Union, Mondays at Mayberry, attending concerts in the mini dome and sporting events; the SU experience is like no other. No matter where you go, if you meet a SU alumnus, you instantly become family.

With dreams of playing sports in college, Southern University afforded me that opportunity. Southern's nurturing environment stimulated my confidence, sharpened my interpersonal skills, and gave me the opportunity to explore the vast possibilities that the world has to offer. Southern University definitely prepares you to excel in any environment. Attending SUBR left me with a large collection of lifelong baseball brothers and friends.

Upon graduating, I knew I wanted to develop a support program for kids which promotes youth sport participation and healthy development. Therefore, I established "Vision of Champions," which is a network supporting children and teens to achieve their greatest potential, on the court, on the field, and in life. I am currently a locomotive engineer for Union Pacific Railroad. Presently, my wife (Sharlene) and I reside in Baytown, Texas. In 2018, I was a recipient in the Southern University Alumni Association Inaugural 40 Under forty class. During my years at Southern University, my college education prepared me for a smooth transition from school to work by providing me with the skills necessary to succeed.

I am blessed to have had the college experience I had, and I always look forward to returning to the campus that became my home away from home.

About Belfred "TJ" Pryer, Jr.

Belfred Pryer Jr., better known as TJ, graduated from Southern University A&M College in 2011 with a Bachelor of Science degree in Business Management and Entrepreneurship and he is the founder of Vision of Champions. While at Southern University, TJ was a Pitcher on the 2009 SWAC Baseball Championship Team under the leadership of Hall of Fame Coach Roger Cador. He's currently a Locomotive Engineer for Union Pacific and held the title of youngest Black Employee Network President for 2 successful terms. His Vision of Champions organization is dedicated to motivating and inspiring the youth, providing scholarships and resources through youth sports.

ARIA N. GROSS

Living Legend
Aria N. Gross

Who am I?

I am the proud daughter of two Southern University graduates, but little did I know that the bonds they created would be the blueprint of a legacy in the making. Not only am I the product of Southern legacy but my grandmother Mary B. Matthews worked faithfully for Southern University for over 37 years as Housing Supervisor and a distinguished member of the SU Housing Department. Southern legacy runs deep in my family as my aunts and cousin also attended Southern University. Although my older sister Mindy did not attend Southern University, she graduated from Alabama A&M where she was a cheerleader and captain of the Dancing Divas.

Now let me take you on a journey of who I am.

Growing up my family moved around a lot. I was born at Women's Hospital in Baton Rouge, LA in 1987, but only a short two years passed before my family moved to Topeka, KS where my dad completed his doctorate degree at Kansas State University. In 1992 my family then moved to Nashville, TN where my mom and dad accepted job offers at Tennessee State University. We lived in Nashville, TN for about 10 years then in 2001 my family moved to West Chester, PA where my dad worked at Cheyney University (the first HBCU).

As a young child growing up, I was exposed to the HBCU culture at an early age. My fondest memories as a young girl was going back to Louisiana to attend Southern University's Homecoming and Bayou Classic with my mom and dad. I was fascinated with the sounds of the Human Jukebox band, the Fabulous Dancing Dolls, the Greek show and the overall southern hospitality. It was just something about the energy I felt being among the students and alumni that made me more eager to attend an HBCU.

Fast forward to my senior year in high school, where I had to make the biggest decision…what college did I want to attend?

Now I had applied to other colleges and universities, but my mind said follow your heart…so it was a no brainer that Southern University was always in my heart. And as the saying goes "home is where the heart is" and that's exactly where I felt at home, back in Baton Rouge, LA.

August 2005 was the beginning of my Southern University experience. I will never forget my first week of my freshman year. I was so excited to be on campus and enjoy college life not realizing the magnitude of the most devastating Hurricane was only miles away… Hurricane Katrina. Shortly after unpacking my bags and getting settled into the dorms, I remember the campus shutting down and telling students to evacuate. I remember going to my grandmother's house in Baker, LA to be with her while the storm passed.

Although the devastation of one of the worst hurricanes in history occurred, I did not let that deter me from my studies and college journey. During my four years at Southern University, I became active in the student body by volunteering with several organizations, joined the women's track team, served as Executive Assistant to the Sophomore Class President (SGA), was a contributing writer/reporter for the school newspaper *The Digest*, and a Peer Health Educator all while staying on the Dean's List every semester.

I also served as President of the Public Relations Student Society of America at Southern University. I was blessed to have an opportunity to intern at Turner Entertainment Networks in Atlanta, GA in the public relations department. I give credit to my professors in the Mass Communications department for challenging and mentoring me. It was the close-knit community and family-like environment that I experienced that allowed me to feel that I could achieve anything to which I set my mind and heart.

While attending Southern University I met my college sweetheart and my now husband Brandon. It's funny because I look back on how my parents met. My dad was elected SGA president and my mom was his campaign manager. I developed relationships with friends that I now consider my family and gained an experience of a lifetime.

In the spring of 2007, I became a member of the Alpha Tau chapter of Delta Sigma Theta Sorority, Inc. which was a special moment for me because my mom and my aunt were both also initiates of the Alpha Tau chapter of Delta Sigma Theta Sorority, Inc., making me a legacy. As a young girl growing up I strived to be just like my mom and aunt…focused, determined and a leader…the true epitome of a Delta woman.

I was honored to be selected as Miss Junior for 2007-2008. It was a privilege to be a part of the distinguished Royal Court and becoming a class queen was such an amazing experience. During my reign as Miss Junior, I was involved in many public service activities including fundraising for St. Jude's Children Research hospital, volunteering in the Campus-wide clean up, and participating in food drives during Thanksgiving to help underprivileged families during the holidays. To me it was more than just wearing a crown and parading around at football games. It taught me humility and that we serve a greater purpose which is to give back to our communities and leave a lasting impression with those you encounter.

As I walked across the stage my senior year in 2009, I didn't know what the future held for my life after college, but I did know that I left behind a legacy…I am and will forever be a Proud legacy Jag!

As the great poet and author Maya Angelou said, "If you're going to live, leave a legacy. Make a mark on the world that can't be erased."

So, what will your legacy be?

About Aria N. Gross

Aria Gross was born in Baton Rouge, Louisiana and raised in Nashville, Tennessee. In the middle of her Freshman year in high school she moved to West Chester, Pennsylvania, but after high school she made her way back to her Southern roots.

Aria's mother, father and aunts all attended and graduated from Southern University. Her grandmother faithfully worked for Southern University Housing Department from 1946 to 1983, so it was only right for her continue the Southern tradition.

She graduated Spring 2009 with her Bachelor's degree in Mass Communications with a concentration in Public Relations from Southern University and A&M College in Baton Rouge, LA.

While at Southern University Aria was a member of the Women's Track team, she served as the Executive Assistant to the Sophomore Class President, Contributing Writer for the school newspaper The Digest, Miss Junior 2007-2008 (Southern University Royal Court), and a Spring 2007 initiate of the Alpha Tau Chapter of Delta Sigma Theta Sorority, Inc.

Aria currently works in the Insurance industry as a Property Homeowners Adjuster in the Los Angeles area.

She is the wife of Brandon K. Gross (her college sweetheart) and mother of two boys Christian and Dillon Gross.

In her free time she enjoys traveling, spending time with her family, volunteering with her sons sports activities and caring for her dog, Enzo.

CHRISTOPHER NETTER-MOSES

The Power of the Circle
Christopher Netter-Moses

My experience at Southern University would not be considered unusual or spectacular, but it is different from most. Throughout my high school years, counselors rarely, if ever, encouraged students to attend a Historically Black College or University. My mother and father both attended Southern University and Agricultural & Mechanical College in Baton Rouge, LA for a short time, but outside of the Bayou Classic, they never really addressed their experiences on campus with me. While in high school, I participated in Upward Bound at Xavier University of Louisiana, which was essential in introducing me to HBCUs and ultimately led to my decision to attend Southern University.

Southern University provided me with some of the most memorable experiences of my life, including sporting events, President Obama's election celebration, and real-world experiences on The Yard. I traveled with the university, which is where I met my future wife. I've made lasting friends and developed lifelong partnerships. Most importantly, I graduated from what is, in my opinion, the greatest university in the world.

Everyone who attended an HBCU believes that their university is the best ever, and that sense of pride enhances the HBCU experience. We have a strong attachment to our universities, both in good and bad times. That pride is difficult to find elsewhere; it is one of the few things that we as black people still have, so we cherish it.

In the Fall of 2008, I enrolled at Southern University; it was my first time away from home, but I quickly felt at home. I was now in a structured atmosphere where black people predominated and culture was valued. There were young individuals from many walks of life and origins who looked exactly like me, all with the same objective in mind: to continue our education. Even though we did not all take the same path to graduation, that was the goal. As I walked across campus, I saw a strong sense of community among the students and professors.

In the classroom, the relationship between the professors and students felt genuine. I felt as if the majority of the professors were there for reasons that were more than to simply receive a check. The professors were black men and women who poured into us every single day. They were there to help guide us to become men and women. Courses were designed to force you to think beyond the textbook material, and I learned how to apply those concepts to everyday life.

I lived in the apartments and dormitories in the back of campus during my freshman and sophomore years. During those years, I started to develop my network and spread my wings. Being from New Orleans, Louisiana it's natural for us to stick together once we're out of our environment, so that's exactly what most did once they made it to Baton Rouge. I took it upon myself to meet people from different places, in the wee early hours of the morning. "The Circle" was exactly that, a circle which was in the middle of three dormitory halls located at the back of campus.

The majority of folks would gather in The Circle every day after class to hang around for hours. Most of the time, I would immerse myself in discussions of music, video games, sports (Lebron and The Saints), fashion, and music (Shoutout to The Blog Era). Here, I made new friends from different states and cities that were located in Louisiana that I had never heard of. To this day, some of those friends and I still have those debates.

In my later years of undergrad, I left the circle for underclassmen and moved off of campus, at which time I began to work while attending class. Although working prevented me from being as involved on campus as I would have liked, it was important as adult life started to take hold. But all in all, I was still visible on campus.

The most memorable experience for me on "The Yard" was the evening President Obama won his first election. To experience the first African-American United States President elected while being a student at a Historically Black College and University was an out of body experience to say the least. As cliche as it sounds, it gave us hope and belief that whatever we were set out to achieve while on campus and in life was attainable. We celebrated like none other that night, if I had to guess 90% of the student body was in the circle that night and the only song played for three hours straight was "My President is Black" by Jeezy and I don't remember anyone attending class the next morning, which was counterproductive when I think back on it.

There were undoubtedly certain difficulties that the majority of our beloved colleges suffer, like lengthy wait times for financial aid, housing concerns, scheduling troubles, and various financial difficulties the university and its system had, all of which are the result of underfunding. In hindsight, I'm grateful for each of those difficulties since they taught me how to navigate through life. The saying "if you can make it out of here, you can make it through anything" was popular on campus.

The lesson I took away from my time on "The Yard" that has resonated with me the most is how to adjust to whatever challenges life hands you. For instance, throughout my time there, the university saw numerous funding reductions from the local government. Classes were canceled as a result of the budget cuts, and educators lost their jobs. At one time, the situation got so severe that there were no courses on Fridays at all; as a result, classes were longer during the week, and everyone had to get used to it. The same local government made an attempt to abolish the city bus service, which served as some students' main form of transportation. Students once more needed to adapt. These situations taught me that there is no time to complain in life, when life starts to life it's on you to adapt and adjust.

In conclusion, I believe that attending Southern University was one of the best choices in my life. The experiences both good and bad molded me into the man that I am today. My wife and I met at Southern and ideally my children will attend there as well. I wouldn't alter a thing about my time at Southern University if I had to do it all over again.

About Christopher Netter-Moses

Christopher Netter-Moses is a Louisiana native and has spent his entire life in different cities of its southern region. Today, Christopher serves as a member of the New Orleans Police Department where he enjoys serving the people of New Orleans in their time of need. Christopher was born in Baton Rouge, La and moved to New Orleans at the age of one where he spent the following seventeen years of his life. Christopher enrolled at Southern University and A&M College in Baton Rouge, Louisiana in the Fall 2008 where he obtained a Bachelor's of Science in Criminal Justice.

When not serving the community, he enjoys spending time with his wife and their two sons (and dog). He also enjoys traveling, training and as an admitted sports fanatic, he feeds his addiction by attending and watching the New Orleans Saints, Pelicans and everything Southern.

AUTUMN PAYTON

Raised Resilient
Autumn Payton

As I reminisce about my HBCU experience at Southern University A&M College, I cannot help but feel a profound sense of gratitude for the transformative education and experiences that have shaped me into the person I am today.

Being born and raised in Walker, Louisiana, a small town located in southeastern Louisiana in Livingston Parish, was a challenging experience. Livingston Parish is a predominantly white area, with African Americans comprising 20% of the population. In the 1980s and 1990s, Livingston Parish was the site of several high-profile incidents of racial violence and tension. Growing up as a black girl, in a place that had a complex racial history that dates back to the 19th century, I oftentimes felt isolated and out of place.

Although I lived in Livingston Parish, I lived in a predominately-black neighborhood. This area was my "safe space" around family, friends, and church that instilled values of community, family, and faith were deeply ingrained in me due to living in a small predominately-black area inside of Livingston Parish where I witnessed my grandfather and other black community leaders fight for African Americans voices to be heard. Southern University amplified these values and fostered an environment of black excellence that left an indelible mark on my heart and soul.

My grandparents, first-generation college students and proud alumni of Southern University, instilled within our family a deep appreciation for education and the institution's rich history and legacy.

As I set foot on the vibrant campus at the age of 18, I was immediately immersed in a tapestry of black culture, resilience, and brilliance that not only provided me with an environment for academic growth but also fostered a sense of community and belonging that I had never experienced before.

I experienced a bit of a culture shock. Suddenly, I found myself in an environment where black students, professors, and staff members are leading, excelling, and inspiring. It was empowering, but also surprising since I hadn't been exposed to such representation before. For me, seeing accomplished professionals who looked like me and were trailblazers in their own fields was a stark contrast to my previous experiences.

The vibrant energy that coursed through the veins of the campus was palpable, and it infused me with a profound sense of pride, not just in my personal accomplishments, but also in the history, legacy, and achievements of the black community as a whole.

From the dynamic and thought-provoking conversations with my fellow classmates to the inspiring and tireless efforts of the faculty and staff, the entire Southern University community embraced me with open arms, and I knew that I had found a place where I could thrive both personally and academically.

Stewart Hall, the Mass Communications building at Southern University, holds a special place in my heart. It was more than just a building or a place to attend classes; it was a home away from home.

Dr. Fuller's Communications law class stood out as the most formidable challenge among all the courses in the mass communications program at Southern University A&M College. Ask any mass comm student, and they would attest to the rigor and demanding nature of this class, which was an essential requirement for graduation. Throughout the semester, this class brought forth a series of formidable challenges, pushing each student to their limits. The intricacies of media law, regulations, and ethical considerations posed complex hurdles that demanded relentless effort and dedication to navigate successfully. However, amidst the academic struggle, something remarkable happened – the class brought the students together in a shared mission to conquer one of the most daunting courses in the program. Collaborative study sessions, group discussions, and collective brainstorming became the norm as classmates sought to support and uplift one another. The class forged a bond among mass communications majors, instilling a sense of camaraderie and resilience that extended far beyond the confines of Dr. Fuller's classroom.

As difficult as it was, this class became a defining experience for all, shaping not only their understanding of communications law but also their ability to work as a cohesive team to overcome seemingly insurmountable challenges.

The faculty members at Southern University were not just educators, but mentors, advocates, and champions of their student's success who focused on developing students into professionals.

This was a refreshing change from my previous academic experiences in Walker, where many teachers seemed disinterested in the growth of black students.

The professors at Southern University invested their time, knowledge, and unwavering support to ensure the intellectual development of their students. They went above and beyond to help students secure internships that would nurture their professional growth, and they reaffirmed their worth with every explanation and reassurance. Through their tireless efforts, the faculty members at Southern University helped my peers and I grow into confident and capable professionals, ready to take on the world.

The bonds forged with like-minded African-American students at Southern University were equally instrumental in shaping my journey. Friendships blossomed, solidifying a support network that transcended the academic realm.

My college experience was enriched not only by the friendships I formed but also by the strong sense of family that emerged within my circle. Navigating the campus together, my friends and I shared countless moments of laughter, sadness, commiseration, and inspiration, forming bonds that felt like the ties of kinship.

This feeling of family was further strengthened by the presence of my older cousins who were already students at Southern and warmly welcomed me with open arms. Their guidance and support were invaluable, making me feel at home in my environment.

As the days passed, our group of friends became inseparable, and our gatherings became cherished traditions. Mondays were marked by the indulgence of "red bean Monday" and "Catfish Friday" in Mayberry, while Wednesdays at noon were reserved for our regular meetups at the Union on "Pretty Wednesdays." These moments were the highlights of the week, fostering a sense of unity.

The feeling of family extended even further as more of my cousins joined the campus in subsequent years, expanding our family and friendship circle, creating an even more vibrant and supportive community. Throughout our college journey, our friends became more than just companions; they became an extension of our family, shaping our experiences and leaving a lasting impact on our lives beyond graduation.

Graduate school at Southern University was yet another facet of this remarkable journey at this institution. This time around, our professors regarded us as adults, fully capable of harnessing our potential and embracing the responsibilities that lay before us. Reuniting with college friends within the classroom walls, we embarked on this new phase of our academic journey, pooling our collective knowledge, wisdom, and experiences.

Today, I owe much of my success to the resilience instilled within me, the unwavering determination to defy the odds, and an unyielding spirit that refuses to accept defeat. Southern University

A&M College has not only provided me with an exceptional academic foundation but also nourished my cultural identity and imbued me with a deep sense of purpose and social responsibility.

Southern University has taught me that education is not just about acquiring knowledge; it is about shaping one's character, building relationships, and positively impacting the world. It has empowered me to pursue my dreams and believe that anything is possible with hard work, perseverance, and faith.

The friendships and connections I formed at Southern University A&M College have remained a vital pillar of support contributing to my continued success. Even after graduation, the bonds we established during our college years have transcended time and distance, proving to be enduring and impactful.

Through the highs and lows of post-grad life, my Southern University friends have been there to celebrate achievements, offer encouragement during challenges, and provide a sense of belonging that transcends physical location. Together, we navigate the complexities of adulthood, each bringing our unique experiences and perspectives to the table, enriching our lives and propelling us forward. As we pursue our respective careers and dreams, we remain united by the shared experiences and values instilled in us during our time at Southern University.

It is through these genuine friendships that I find strength and inspiration, grateful for the unwavering support system that continues to shape and elevate my journey long after our days on campus. Southern University will forever hold a special place in my heart, not only as the place where I received an exceptional education but as the home where I found lifelong friendships that continue to foster personal and professional growth.

As I continue to navigate life's journey, I carry the lessons and values I gained from this remarkable institution, forever grateful for the pivotal role it played in shaping the person I am today.

About Autumn Payton

Autumn Payton, native of Walker, Louisiana holding two degrees from Southern University in Baton Rouge, she is a skilled communicator with a bachelor's degree in Mass Communications-Broadcast Journalism and a master's degree in Public Administration-Public Policy.

Currently, Autumn serves as the Assistant Chief of Communications for the City of Baton Rouge under Mayor-President Sharon Weston Broome's administration. But her career in communications began in 2014 when she joined the Livingston Parish Sheriff's Office as a Public Information Officer for both the Livingston Parish Sheriff's Office and the Twenty-First Judicial District Attorney's Office. There, she honed her skills in content creation, writing, producing, and publishing news on court cases, crime, and community events, including the 2016 flood devastation in Livingston Parish.

After several years in public service, Autumn's passion for content creation and social media led her back to the news world. In 2021, she worked as the WAFB+ executive producer, serving as a digital reporter and producer.

Beyond her professional accomplishments, Autumn is dedicated to her community. She spends her free time organizing community events with Club Outreach, a non-profit organization in her hometown of Walker. When she's not working or volunteering, you can find her enjoying leisure activities such as spending quality time with her husband Jay Colar, whom she met at Southern University, working out at the gym, or enjoying brunch with loved ones.

MYLISHA ROBINSON, J.D.

"I am TENACIOUS"
Mylisha Robinson, J.D.

What makes me so special to become a part of this book? What have I accomplished that makes me so unique? What can I truly offer? I didn't complete four years here. These are the thoughts that have run through my mind as I contemplated what I would write. However, the truth of the matter is I never gave up despite my circumstances.

Mylisha Rae Robinson, J.D., a thirty-year-old mother of two from Baton Rouge, Louisiana graced the campus of Southern University in her early 20s in Fall of 2013. I grew up in a two-parent household with one older brother. My parents were what you consider working class individuals. My mom worked at Blue Cross Blue Shield of Louisiana and my dad worked at The Advocate production plant and operated his own lawn and landscaping business. Neither of my parents have a four-year college degree, however my dad did obtain his associate degree from Southern University. This university had been embedded deep inside my roots from an early age. I can recall going to several football games on campus with my parents. My dad was sure to have me with a pair of jeans fresh from the cleaners starched down, SU flags attached to the windows and my shakers to cheer on the team.

From the outside looking in, I grew up in a typical household and didn't have any problems but oh that's far from the truth. I found myself placed in the center of situations that were often overwhelming. The older you get the more you start to see things for what they are and the things that didn't make sense as a child now you understand.

Throughout my school years, I maintained good grades, I was a scholar student that consistently maintained honor roll status. My daddy preached that my only job was school, no matter what else was going on my education was first. I don't consider myself a problem child but a child that weighed her options, if it was something I wanted to do, there wasn't anything that could stop me.

When it was time to apply for college, I only applied to one school and was accepted but unfortunately it was not THEE SOUTHERN UNIVERSITY. I wanted to get away from Baton Rouge, I needed new scenery, I wanted to run away from the drama at home. However, after two years away I finally found my way to the YARD. I found out I was pregnant over winter break and decided it was best to come home because all of my help was here in Baton Rouge. The transition home was hard for me from the family drama that I originally ran from to being in a different space with the person I was having a child for. I was due early September, so that meant I couldn't wait until the last minute to have my stuff together. Therefore, I spent the summer months back and forth on campus making sure everything from financial aid to my class schedule was in place for the first day of classes. It was imperative for me that I stayed on track to finish my degree within the next two years. My line sister often reminds me of how she remembers seeing me waddling around campus that summer. Y'all it was a HOT summer, and I was HUGE.

August came and classes began. From day one, I made it a point to personally meet one on one with my professors, making them aware of my due date and to see if they would work with me. Fortunately, I encountered some understanding professors. I was ultimately concerned about being in class long enough to receive my financial aid without any problems. Luckily, I delivered my baby girl on September 4, 2013, just a short while after the date that needed to be met. I was out exactly six weeks before returning to campus and when I came back it was right before homecoming. And for the most part I went to class and went home but I did occasionally pop my head out to a few events. The football team was on fire this season, we won the Bayou Classic and then went on to Houston to win the 2013 SWAC Championship. My first semester on the YARD went swiftly but I can truly say I don't regret coming home.

I was on a mission; it was always a dream to pledge the greatest sorority there is and being home to pledge this specific chapter would mean that much more. On April 23, 2014, I was allotted the privilege of becoming a member of the Alpha Tau Chapter of Delta Sigma Theta Sorority Incorporated. I stepped out of my comfort zone and ran for an office position after becoming a member of the sorority and was elected recording secretary for the chapter. Because of Southern University and Delta Sigma Theta, I was introduced to what I consider "My Village", a group of women that I didn't know I needed and can honestly say I don't know if I could manage life without them now.

Southern University welcomed me with open arms my first year there and I can truly say I was happy to be there. I was a Mass Communications major with a focus in Public Relations. I am a person that does not care to be the center of attention; therefore, I pursued a degree that was impactful but allowed me to be in the background pushing things forward.

At the start of my senior year, I was adamant to move out of my parents' home by the time my daughter made one. I had once again placed myself on a timeline. I felt that if I had a child then it was my responsibility to provide for her without the conditions of others. I tend to be very hard on myself. I was able to move into my apartment in early October 2014.

We often make plans for ourselves in how we want our lives to go but then something comes and turns your world upside down. I forced myself to come home because of my pregnancy and was blessed with a village to help raise her. My parents were going through a separation when I came home so that was a big adjustment. It wasn't a surprise, but it was a lot. I was placed in the middle of two people I loved dearly all while dealing with pregnancy emotions and pursuing a degree. However, let's fast forward back to October 2014. I was enrolled in Dr. Fuller's class and if you're familiar with the Mass Communications department then you know she wasn't the easiest class to pass. During this time, I was working on a research paper and my mom had been complaining of pain in her stomach that wouldn't go away. One evening she went to the emergency room and was told she needed to have surgery to remove her gallstones. After the gallstones were removed, the family was informed we needed to come to the hospital and at this time I was notified that my mom had stage four colon cancer. My heart broke because my thoughts were stage four doesn't go away, so what exactly does this mean? I wasn't familiar with colon cancer at the time, so I honestly didn't know what came next.

Also, during this fabulous month of October, I found out I was pregnant with my second child shortly after receiving the news of my mom. I thought of the old tale old folks use to reference when someone close passes away someone is born. So, in my mind my mom would soon pass away because I was pregnant. However, that didn't exactly happen that way. Luckily enough for me my mom was able to start chemotherapy and witness me graduate with my bachelor's degree May 2015.

At times I feel I shortened my college experience because I entered Southern pregnant and graduated pregnant. However, my circumstances made me uncomfortable which gave me the driving force to keep going. Although I tried to run, SOUTHERN UNIVERSITY is and will forever be home. I come from a family of Southern University graduates ranging from the College of Business to the Engineering Department.

After a back-and-forth battle, my mom transitioned August 16, 2016. I saw it coming and I told myself I would be ok because it hurt like hell to see her suffer and not be able to take the pain away. I honestly didn't know what was next, but I knew my current position wasn't my final position. My goal was to provide stability and security for my daughters, I vowed to be someone they could be proud of. It was heavy on my mind to go back to school, but I wasn't sure what I wanted to go for. I was currently working in a law firm and knew a handful of attorneys, so I was weighing my options of either law school or going for my master's degree. Ultimately, I wanted flexibility within my career and the ability to grow and be afforded endless opportunities. Thus, I decided to give law school a try and what better place to go than to Thee Southern University Law Center.

My law school education started August 2018 two years after the death of my mom. I was accepted into the part-time day program and completed my degree over the course of four years in December of 2022. Over the course of four years, I experienced death of close friends and family, the pandemic, stressful living conditions, family members in jail, and financial struggles. Honestly it's not much I can say I didn't go through. Law school was a different speed and a challenge within itself. There were days when I cried, I second guessed myself and I thought about throwing in the towel, but I didn't. Tears fell but I kept fighting, there was no plan b, I had no choice. The Southern University System gave me family, made me utilize my networking skills and gave me the resources to get things done. You can't be afraid to ask for help, the resources are there and if they aren't there, there are people that will help you find them. When I think I'm in the clear and will experience something without fighting several battles I'm consistently shown differently.

As I prepare to take the July 2023 Louisiana Bar Exam, I'll leave you with this. I have only scratched the surface and have yet to reach my full potential, remember my name because this won't be your last time hearing of me. I am just getting started. There hasn't been a challenge I have not overcome. My advice to the next person that feels the weight of the world is on their shoulder is to stand strong and take care of you. Don't be so hard on yourself, enjoy the moment and live your life, what's for you is FOR YOU and will be there when it's time. The road won't always be easy, but you will overcome it. Don't be afraid to ask for help because there are people you don't know rooting for you.

About Mylisha Robinson, J.D.

Mylisha R. Robinson, J.D. is a thirty-year-old native of Baton Rouge, La., and a two-time graduate of the Southern University System. Mylisha obtained her bachelor's degree in mass communications from Southern University A & M College in 2015 and recently obtained her Doctor of Jurisprudence from the Southern University Law Center in 2022. Mylisha is currently studying to become a licensed attorney in the state of Louisiana while juggling the role of being a full-time mother and full-time employee.

She is the mother of two beautiful daughters ages seven and nine and currently employed with the Louisiana Workforce Commission at the Office of Worker's Compensation as a Workforce Compliance Analyst I in the Records Management division. Mylisha looks at the reality of what life throws us, the good, the bad and the ugly and no matter what, she is determine to beat all odds, she's determine to be successful.

SASHA BROUSSARD

The Lessons in the Losses
Sasha Broussard

Introduction to HBCUs

When asked to write about my Historically Black College and University experience, deciding on a story, an experience, or starting point was tricky. My first memory of Southern University is no longer a memory; it is a collection of experiences. I cannot recollect my first memory because so many of them are fond—almost magical. My mother, Sharon Roussell Steib, is the first person who introduced this phenomenal Historically Black College and University to my sister and I. Hearing stories from my mother, who attended Southern University from 1980 – 1985, was the highlight of our drives to Baton Rouge, Louisiana. The stories transitioned into dressing in our blue and gold and tailgating with family and friends before Saturday night football games in A.W. Mumford Stadium. As a child, I thought this was typical for all families: regular bonding time and a part of our regular schedule because we never missed a game!

As I reflect upon those years, I now know it was all intentional. It was my mother intentionally exposing us to Historical Black Colleges and Universities. Not only did we learn about Southern University, but we visited and learned about other HBCUs. My mother was deliberate about instilling the importance of HBCUs and the significance those colleges and universities played in our community. Growing up in Vacherie, Louisiana, there were few African Americans, and even fewer who had the opportunity to attend college. My mother made it clear that attending college was not an option. As an adolescent, I thought Southern University was my only option, but my mother allowed my sister and I to apply wherever we wanted to go. Being familiar with Southern, I wanted a different experience, so I applied to other HBCUs and Predominantly White Institutions

(PWIs). However, before attending Jaguar Preview, I had planned to attend another HBCU, but God said otherwise.

God's imagination always remains wider than our human imagination.

I enrolled at Southern University in August 2005. The summer before starting, I attended Jaguar Preview; I made a few new friends and knew some people from Vacherie who were already attending the University, but I did not have any close friends going to Southern. I had attended a private, predominately white Catholic High School, and none of my friends from high school were attending Southern University. When I got settled into Southern, I realized that was the case for most first-year students. One of the first people I connected with was an upperclassman, and he was such a tremendous help getting me acclimated with financial aid and helping me get into a dormitory. We still have a friendship today, and I will always be grateful for his help throughout my college years. As I began to forge more friendships and my first lessons at Southern University arose, I knew that if I was going to be successful here, I needed to have a support system and remain positive. I have always been outgoing, but I was shy and unsure of myself as a young adult.

Upon arriving on campus, I was encouraged by a longtime friend and upperclassman to run for Miss Freshman. I started my campaign with the few friends I made at Jaguar Preview and some friends I already knew. I did not win Miss Freshman, but campaigning helped me meet new people and brought me closer to my new friend group. It was amazing having the support of my new friends. They believed in me and having those experiences with them brought us closer. That first year brought some losses, such as trying out for the dancing dolls and not winning Miss Freshman. But I took the good out of each setback and looked at the positive from each situation. God's imagination was broader than I ever imagined, and I would not change any of those losses.

A loss isn't a loss if you learn something because of it.

During my remaining years attending Southern, I had more losses, but they pale in comparison to my successes and blessings. If a stranger were to look in on my life, it would be easy for them to say that I have had many opportunities handed to me. Since I come from a two–parent, middle–class household, yes things were a little easier for me, but I have always worked hard, and my parents have always taught my sister and I the importance of having a strong work ethic. And work hard I did—for EVERYTHING I have: every grade, every dollar, every degree.

In the Fall of 2006, I decided to major in Political Science with a goal of applying to law school after graduating. However, this desire changed by the Spring of 2007, and I transferred to the College of Business (T.T. Allain) to major in Marketing. To catch up and remain on my graduation timeline, I took Principles of Management and Principles of Marketing in the Summer of 2007. At this point, I had to apply for student loans because the Louisiana TOPS program did not cover my summer school expenses. This decision was a massive challenge because I already started taking political science classes and had to take introductory level College of Business courses to remain on track to graduate by the Spring of 2009. At the end of Fall 2007, the Business major turned out differently than I intended. My current GPA dropped from 3.5 to 2.6 in just one semester after transferring to the College of Business. I remember thinking to myself, more losses, and these losses were tremendous because my grade point average was affected.

Nevertheless, there was always someone for me to lean on at the College of Business, including peers and professors. Being involved in the college helped me to find that support and get my footing in a new major that was vastly different from my previous aspiration. The support that I and so many other students receive is a huge benefit of an HBCU. I not only gained knowledge via academics, but I learned from people who really cared about me. The strategies boosted my confidence and enabled me to overcome barriers, to aim high, and to succeed. To reiterate, I learned that early on with the help of the College of Business and I began to get back on track. By the end of Spring 2008, my GPA was climbing back up, and after taking more summer classes during the Summer 2008, my GPA was back at 3.5. I may have lost some GPA points, but I learned so much more while attending the College of Business.

Instilling the HBCUs

Although I did not become a dancing doll or Miss Freshman, I was not deterred. That HBCU "can-do spirit" and my mom's (parents') lessons were instilled in me. So, I tried out for the Gold N Bluez dance team and was a part of the team from 2005 to 2007. Lastly, I ran for Miss Senior and was a part of the 2008-2009 Royal Court. After the trials I experienced with my GPA, I graduated in Spring 2009 with a GPA above 3.0. Southern University allowed me to never give up and provided me other opportunities to thrive and succeed. I formed lasting personal, educational, and professional bonds. I benefited from mentors who believed in me and my talents and abilities. I was in a nurturing, yet demanding environment that let me be my best self.

I will continue instilling the importance of HBCUs in my family, as my mother intentionally instilled it in my sister and I. My daughter attended Homecoming and Bayou Classic before the age of one. She already bleeds Blue and Gold as she waves her mini pom-poms. This is the start of her HBCU experience, even if she decides to attend Southern University, another HBCU, or PWI. She will know these institutions' importance to people like her grandmother and mother. Everyone has their own HBCU experience. Family, wins, and losses are a part of my HBCU experience, and as I reflect on my journey, each loss has molded me into the wins I have today.

About Sasha Broussard

Sasha Steib Broussard began her collegiate career at Southern University A&M College in Baton Rouge, Louisiana, in the Fall of 2005, after graduating from Ascension Catholic High School in Donaldsonville, Louisiana. The Vacherie, Louisiana, native soon became involved in and assumed leadership positions in numerous organizations, such as the Student Government Association and the Gold N' Bluez dance team. Becoming a Fall 2007 initiate of the Beta Psi Chapter of Alpha Kappa Alpha Sorority, Inc., and serving on the Royal Court as Miss Senior 2008-2009 were highlights of an impactful four years at one of the premier HBCU's in the nation.

While attending Southern University, Sasha started working part-time in the hospitality industry. After graduating from the College of Business with a B.S. in Marketing, she continued working in sales for various hospitality brands such as Marriott, Hyatt, and Hilton. This career path took her to Chicago, Illinois, and then back to Louisiana to work in the Cultural Capital of the South, New Orleans, and to have her fingers on the pulse of numerous events and interact with individuals and organizations that came to the city.

Sasha's desire to learn more about business led her to apply to Louisiana State University Flores Master of Business Administration program, which she completed in 2015. Armed with her MBA degree, she remained in the hospitality industry until 2020, when she transitioned into working in the family businesses: Greater Louisiana Insurance Group, NAMELOC Trucking, and Greater Louisiana Real Estate. Being an entrepreneur has always been a goal for Sasha and supporting her family by assisting her husband Robert Broussard Jr. in operating their insurance agency has been a dream. Sasha is looking forward to growing the family businesses with her husband, hoping to leave a legacy for their children to continue.

An active member of the Phi Sigma Omega Chapter of Alpha Kappa Alpha Sorority, Inc., Sasha resides in New Orleans, Louisiana, with her husband, Robert, and daughter Savannah Marie.

ALLIESHA LEGARDE

A Professional Pursuit
Alliesha LeGarde

In the words of Brene Brown, "One day, you will tell your story of how you overcame what you went through, and it will be someone else's survival guide." My time is now. I was born in Hammond, Louisiana, a smaller city where everyone knows everyone, in a neighborhood where community meant a lot to the residents. People were always willing to lend a helping hand. I was raised by my mom, a single mother who showered me with so much love and affection. Although, as an adolescent, I considered myself to be both shy and reserved, I wouldn't say I liked to interact with other children my age. I just wanted to be under my mom. One would say that I was a "mommy's girl" and still am to this day. The woman I am now is a product of my mother's nurturing. I had an ordinary upbringing. She taught her children to be honest, work hard, and dream big.

There are several of her traits that I recognize in myself. I take pride in my work and always do my best. My dedication to finishing what I start is one of my defining traits. As a kid, I observed how hard my mom worked to provide for my siblings and I. It sparked a passion within me. I convinced myself I wasn't a by-product of my upbringing. What was going on in the world around me became clear to me. One's path of perseverance, drive, and a refusal to be defined by one's circumstances begins when one chooses to make a better life for themselves despite starting with nothing. It's evidence of the resilience of the human spirit and our capacity to break through barriers. "I came from nothing" is commonly used to describe someone who has had a difficult start in life. It could indicate having a difficult childhood, such as being raised in poverty or a hostile environment. However, those who pursue their aspirations rather than giving up or accepting their lot in life set off on a path of transformation. Having a specific goal in mind and an unwavering commitment to reaching it are essential first steps to a better life. With this goal of wanting a better life, I was inspired to act and make positive changes. It serves as a driving force, encouraging people to make positive changes and persevere despite setbacks.

When you're on the brink of poverty, you may feel an overwhelming urge to improve your situation. Throughout my childhood, this was my reality. The thirst lighted a fire within, motivating me to put in the time, energy, and effort required to make change happen. I had so much confidence in myself that I refused to accept mediocrity and strive for continuous improvement. The road from poverty to prosperity is rarely smooth or easy. There were several obstacles to overcome and times of uncertainty. These tests, however tricky, helped me mature into a more assertive, more resilient person. Every setback was a chance to learn and improve; each defeat was a building block for future success. Aspiration becomes a formative process that molds the achiever and the achieved goal. Individuals on this road must frequently accept and even welcome uncertainty. I knew I needed to upskill, find a mentor or an educational opportunity, or connect with like-minded people who could help me achieve my goals. It included working long hours, juggling many jobs, and dealing with criticism and rejection. But if I wanted a better life, I had to be willing to put in the work and put up with the pain now to reap the rewards afterward.

When I was 15, I got my first job. I was a medical assistant in a little clinic. I worked a total of eight hours, five days a week, in the office. If you saw me as a teenager, you may have assumed I was doing it to fund my wardrobe. But the truth is that I did it to support my loved ones. My mother had to be on bed rest for her pregnancy with my younger sister. She could hardly move, and though she attempted to hide it behind her warm and beautiful smile, I could see the misery in her eyes. Even as a kid, I was close to my mom. There were occasions when she anticipated my next thought or finished my phrases. So, I encouraged her to rely on me for her needs. I worked all summer long, eight hours a day, five days a week, to ensure my family had a place to live and food.

My life has been defined between working and continuing my education. I was always one of the best students in my class since I loved reading and learning when I was young. I was one of the top students in my eighth-grade class and one of the top in my twelfth-grade class. After finishing high school, I studied business management at Southern University A & M College. I had yet to settle on a concentration for my undergraduate studies in business, and it would be too time-consuming to isolate one specific facet of the business world. My only clue was that I found business classes exciting and was eager to learn more. I am always interested in discovering new ways to broaden my awareness of the business world and learning about its many facets. Southern University and A&M College awarded me a Master of Business Administration degree in December 2017.

After finishing my master's degree, I needed some time off to recharge my batteries, so I took it. Since I was 15, I'd been working and attending school full-time, and I could feel it taking a toll on my health. In 2020, a global pandemic struck. I used this time to consider the following steps I needed to take to reach my new objectives. The search for a Doctor of Business Administration (DBA) degree began. The Doctor of Business Administration program at Liberty University, where I intend to study strategic management, has admitted me. I am in the research phase of my doctoral program now. I have been working to advance my career while continuing my studies.

I work as a Workday Consultant at one of the leading IT companies. Currently, I am responsible for technological and functional design and software distribution. Workday is an HR management platform, and I have my certification. As a Workday Consultant, I am responsible for relaying specific contextual details. The work sessions I've led in the past have given me the experience

I need to examine the reporting needs of businesses. Because of this, I can now help clients with intricate business issues within their own company. As part of my responsibilities, I operate as a point of contact for our clients and use prototypes to showcase several design directions. As a result, the customer now better understands how to use the system effectively. I attend customer meetings to collect and record information for company growth purposes. I used the Workday framework's configuration features to construct and administer the application. I've been a part of the Workday community for over four years. This position challenges me intellectually and allows me to regularly explore my limits within the system. This work is now a profession rather than a job. It combines two of my strengths: interest and competence. I had only a hazy idea of working with computers. I was working in banking for several years and worked on enhancing my customer service skills. One day, a friend of mine asked me if she could refer me for a position at her company as they were hiring, and she felt that I possessed the necessary qualifications. I interviewed for the position, and I got the job.

My primary goal in each role was to showcase my abilities fully. Every course has prepared me for this one in its unique way. What would be the one thing that comes up when you ask a former lecturer, manager, or colleague, "What is Alliesha best known for?" They would probably say, "She is helpful, open-minded, aligns her beliefs with the organization's core values, and possesses strong leadership qualities. Her qualities are tenacity, work ethic, organization, and flexibility." This moment in time is best summed up by the adage, "Work hard in silence and let success make the noise." My further education goal is to equip myself better to manage and lead the next generation. Knowledge is strength. I am in a constant state of learning and improvement. The more I take in, the more I can share with others. I've been working on it for a while, but there's still much more to accomplish. Despite everything I have done, I still have a long way to go. Looking at my life from where I am now, you might think I've always been successful, but that's not the case. Despite appearances, my achievement did not happen overnight. No one knew how late I'd work after school to get home in time to study and finish my assignments. I was surprised to find out how many times I had applied for various positions and had been rejected. Every rejection I received only served to fuel my drive. I was aware of my limitations and motivated to overcome them. Due to my exacting standards, I am often my harshest critic. I am well aware of my abilities and the things I have accomplished. When I put my mind to something, I give it my full attention and energy until I succeed.

I said I would share the complete tale at first, but after considering it, I realized that what I said was only the beginning. There is so much more I want to accomplish in this world. I started from nothing and made it through this ordeal, and I have grown immensely from the experience. When you start with little and work hard to achieve your goals, you build a better life for yourself and give others hope that everything is possible. Your experience demonstrates the power of the human will to overcome misfortune and forge a better life for oneself in the face of adversity. They prove the limitless capacity of the human spirit and provide hope to those in a similar position. I plan to keep going as long as possible and accomplish as much as possible. By setting an example, others will feel encouraged and realize they can achieve their goals. Surprises are common in life. I never in a million years would have predicted I'd be where I am now. My professional life is flourishing. I packed up my belongings and bought a new house far from my friends and relatives in a different city. I appreciate everything that has happened to me and the many lessons I have learned. I used to think of obstacles as setbacks, but now I realize they were placed in my path for a reason. In closing, I encourage you to pursue your dreams. There are achievable goals. You can get what you desire if you are willing to put in the effort.

About Alliesha LeGarde

Alliesha is a Workday Consultant who successfully responds to shifting business needs and priorities systematically and effectively. Well-versed in implementing Workday and conducting functional requirements analysis for businesses of all sizes. Focused on functional and technical design and the delivery of software. Certified in Workday HCM, Recruiting, Learning Consulting Core, and Workday Launch. Agile in task management utilizing Azure DevOps, JIRA, and Octane. Outside of work, Alliesha is a Delta Sigma Theta Sorority Inc member who aims to support local communities. She enjoys reading, exercising, and spending time with loved ones in her spare time. Alliesha graduated from Southern University and A&M College with a Master of Business Administration concentration in Human Resources.

According to RP Podcast
CEO/Founder: Ritha Pierre, Esq.
@accordingtorp
accordingtorp@gmail.com

AC Events
The Luxury Planning Experience
CEO/Founder: Amy Agbottah
amy@amycynthiaevents.com

ACTIVate
CEO/Founder: Yladera Drummond, J.D.
contact@activateleadership.org
info@yladeradrummond.com
www.yladeradrummond.com
www.activateleadership.org

AD Bonner Music
CEO/Founder: Adrain Bonner
817-300-3995
adbonnermusic@gmail.com

Allen Financial Solutions
CEO/Founder: Jay Allen
@jay83allen
@Jay Allen
allen.jonathan83@gmail.com

AG Management & Business Consulting
CEO/Founder: Gabriel Langley
www.agmbc.com

The Alli Group, LLC
Real Estate Management
Founders: Lawrence & Nickia Alli
@thealligroupllc
nickia.alli@gmail.com
www.thealligroupllc.com

Alexander G. Events
CEO/Founder: Nathan Alexander Kemp
Nathan A. Kemp, 336-706-1422
Brooke G. Kemp, 336-944-4768
alexgevents20@gmail.com

AMMEA
President: Ernest Stackhouse
ej.stackhouse@gmail.com
www.ammea.org

The Ancestor Key
CEO/Founder: Ja'el Gordon
504-356-1466
theancestor@gmail.com

Ashley Little Enterprises, LLC
CEO/Founder: Dr. Ashley Little
@_ashleyalittle
@Ashley Little
aalittle08@gmail.com
www.ashleylittleenterprises.com

The Self-care Doc
CEO/Founder:
Dr. Raushannah Johnson-Verwayne
Licensed Clinical Psychologist &
Wellness Coach
@Ask Dr RJ
@Ask Dr RJ
www.AskDrRJ.com

Assurance Tax & Accounting Group, LLC
CEO/Founder:
   Kimberlee Collins-Walker
8676 Goodwood Blvd., Ste. 102
Baton Rouge, LA 70876
225-757-7518
kim@assurancetaxbr.com
www.assurancetaxbr.com

Baker & Baker Realty, LLC
CEO/Founder: Christopher Baker
@seedougieblake
@Christopher D. Baker
baker.christopher@gmail.com

Balance Candle Bar
CEO/Founder: Lacey B. Evans
www.shopbalanceco.com

Bald Guys Bake, LLC

CEO/Founder: Torey Searcy

✉ info@baldguysbake.com

www www.baldguysbake.com

BLKWOMENHUSTLE

CEO/Founder: Lashawn Dreher

⌾ @blkwomenhustle

f @Blk Women Hustle

✉ info@blkwomenhustle.com

Beautiful Body & More, LLC

CEO/Founder: Melody Scott

📱 318-716-1507

    318-716-1508 fax

⌾ @Beautifulbodyandmore

f @Beautiful Body & More, LLC

www www.beautifulbodyandmore.com

Block Band Music & Publishing, LLC

CEO/Founder: D. Rashad Watters

📱 919-698-2560

✉ blockbandmusic@gmail.com

The Black Techies/Podcast

CEO/Founder: Herbert L. Seward, III

Where black culture meets the world of technology.

www www.theblacktechies.com

Blue Street Pools

CEO/Founder: Mark Jones

📱 504-502-7655

✉ bluestreetpools@gmail.com

Boardroom Brand, LLC

CEO/Founder: Samuel Brown, III

@_gxxdy

samuel.brown.three@gmail.com

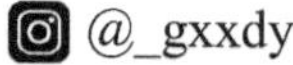

Body to Sole

CEO/Founder: Megan Daniels

225-877-8597

bodytosolefitness@gmail.com

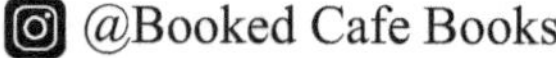

Booked Cafe Books

CEO/Founder: Kierra Jones

@Booked Cafe Books

@Booked Cafe Books

contact@bookedcafebooks.com

www.bookedcafebooks.com

Bound By Conscious Concepts

CEO/Founder: Kathryn Lomax

@msklovibes223

@Klo-Kathryn Lomax

972-638-9823

klomax@bbconcepts.com

Braveheart Medical Mission

CEO/Founder: Erica Rogers

erogers9483@gmail.com

Brooks Art Collective

CEO/Founder: LaToya Brooks

@brooksartcollective

@brooksartcollective

brooksartcollective@gmail.com

BZAR STUDIOZ
CEO/Founder: Steven Baltazar
✉ bzarstudioz@gmail.com
🌐 www.bzarstudioz.com

CAFÉ SAINT-EX
RESTAURANT | BAR

Caleb T. Dunbar Photography
CEO/Founder: Caleb T. Dunbar
📷 @calebtdunbarphotography
f @Caleb T. Dunbar Photography
✉ calebtdunbar@gmail.com
🌐 www.calebtdunbar.com

Campaign Engineers
CEO/Founder: Chris Smith
📷 @csmithatl
✉ csmithl911@gmail.com

Chef Batts
CEO/Founder: Keith Batts
📷 @chefbatts
✉ booking@chefbatts.com

Cici's Freelance Services
CEO/Founder:
   Courtney "Cici" Walker, MPA
📷 @cicisfreelanceservices
📱 225-288-8216
✉ cicisfreelanceservices@gmail.com

Cjenk The Agency: Creative Concierge, LLC

CEO/Founder: Chasmin Jenkins

✉ chasminjenkins@gmail.com

Color Wheel Therapy

CEO/Founder: Kiandra Daniels

☎ 469-251-2418

✉ kiandra.daniels@colorwheeltherapy.com

www www.colorwheeltherapy.com

Commit 2 Life Fitness

CEO/Founder: Joseph T. Shaw III

@ @commit2lifefitness

The Bitter Suite Podcast
Apple & Spotify

@ @thebittersuite2020

www www.commit2life.com

CreativeED Consulting, LLC

CEO/Founder: Dr. William J. Earvin

✉ wjeconsulting@icloud.com

Cultural Resources

CEO/Founder:
  Corey "Mr. Hanky" Dennard

@ @culturalresources

✉ amrhankybeat@gmail.com

Curves & Gains

CEO/Founder: Patrice Murphy

@ @curvesandgaines

✉ curvesandgains@gmail.com

www www.curvesandgains.com

Da Edge 1 Productions

CEO/Founder: Garrett Edgerson

@ @daedge1pro

www www.daedge1pro.com

Daily Life Managements LLC
CEO/Founder:
Kristy Lashaun Burrell
504-390-9949

Dapper Dillon
CEO/Founder: Shaquille Dillon
shaquille.dillon@gmail.com

DD Jones Enterprise
CEO/Founder: Darcele Jones-Horton
darceleh@bellsouth.net

DDL Entertainment
CEO/Founder: Darryl Lassister
darryldlassiter@msn.com

Dee Ree Hair Co
CEO/Founder: Desiree R. Dawson
desireeshanecedawson@yahoo.com

Deroune Services, LLC
CEO/Founder: Marina Zeno
337-418-0785

Dorian Troy Studios
CEO/Founder: Dorian Davis
dorian@doriantroystudios.com

Dr. Ashanti Says, LLC

CEO/Founder: Dr. Ashantia Says

www www.drashantisays.com

www https://linktr.ee/drashantisays

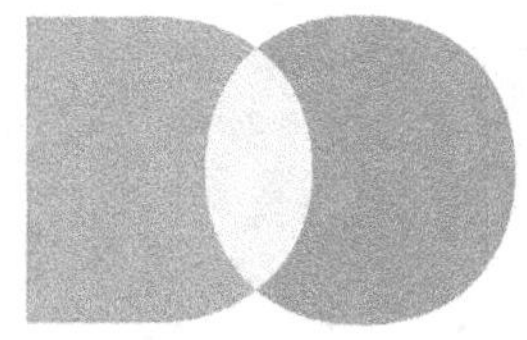

Dream.Org

CEO/Founder: Kasheef Wyzard

@Dream.corps

www www.dream.org

DS National Logistics

CEO/Founder: D. Scott

Scottie.d1911@gmail.com

It's Demi's World Baby Dolls

CEO/Founder: Demi Scott

www www.itsdemisworld.com

Eclectikread Marketing

CEO/Founder: Christa Newkirk

@chris_ta_da

info@eclectikread.com

Elementz4 Designs, LLC

CEO/Founder: Gretta Frierson

www www.elementz4designs.com

www.linktr.ee/elementz4

engHERneered

engHERneered

CEO/Founder: Christina Caldwell, PE

engherneered@gmail.com

Enlightened Visions, Inc.

CEO/Founder: TaNisha Fordham

✉ tanisha.fordham@gmail.com

🌐 www.enlightenedvisions.org

Executive Reign

CEO/Founder: Canisha Cierra Turner

f @Executive Reign

☎ 804-605-6875

🌐 www.executivereign.com

🌐 www.canishacierraturner.com

February First

CEO/Founder: Cedric Livingston

Director/Writer: *February First: A Stride Towards Freedom*

🌐 www.februaryfirstmovie.com

The Flowcus Brand

CEO/Founder: Irone Roussell

📷 @theflowcusbrand

✉ theflowcusbrand.info@gmail.com

🌐 www.theflowcusbrand.com

Freeda's World Podcast

CEO/Founder: Ritha Pierre, Esq.

📷 @freedas_world

✉ accordingtorp@gmail.com

DJ General Mealz

CEO/Founder: Deitrich Armstrong

✉ dtrickarmstrong@gmail.com

Give Black App

Co-Founder/COO: Alexus Hall

 @giveblackapp

 @Give Black App

@giveblackapp

www.giveblackapp.com

Happy Hour Investors

Co-Founder/Managing Partner:
 Jonathan Rivers

830 Glenwood Ave., Ste. 510-352

Atlanta, GA 30316

404-860-2288

jonathan@hhinvestors.com

www.hhinvestors.com

Harbor Institute

CEO/Founder:
 Rasheed Ali Cromwell, J.D.

@theharborinstitute

@The Harbor Institute

@harborinstitute

racromwell@theharborinstitute.com

Harvey Wilder-Foundation

CEO/Founder: Jordan Harvey

www.hawilfoundation.org

HBCU 101

CEO/Founder: Jahliel Thurman

@HBCU101

jahlielthurman@gmail.com

www.hbcu101.com

The HBCU Band Experience with Christy Walker

CEO/Founder: Dr. Christy Walker

christywalker57@gmail.com

www.christywalker.com

The HBCU Experience Movement, LLC

CEO/Founder: Dr. Ashley Little

@_ashleyalittle

@DrAshley Little

thehbcuexperiencemovement@gmail.com

www.thehbcuexperiencemovement.com

HBCU Buzz

(HBCU Buzz | Taper, Inc. | Root Care Health)

CEO/Founder: Luke Lawal, Jr.

@lukelawal

@L & COMPANY

301-221-1719

lawal@lcompany.co

HBCU Girls Talk

CEO/Founder: TeeCee Camper

@HBCUgirlstalk

talkgirls@yahoo.com

HBCU Cheer Black Excellence

@HBCUcheer

HBCUcheerleaders@yahoo.com

HBCU Grad

CEO/Founder: Todd Finley

312-535-8511

www.hbcugraduates.com

HBCU HUB App
connects students directly to HBCUs
CEO/Founder: Dr. Darrius Brooks
 @hbcuhub
www.hbcuhub.us

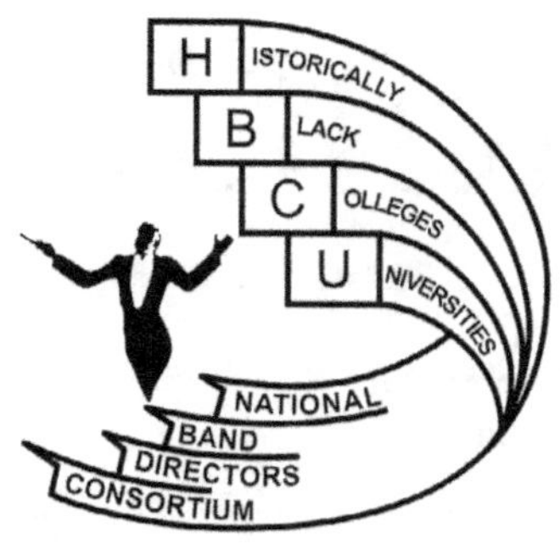

HBCU-NBDOC
www.hbcu-nbdc.org

HBCU Legacy Fashion
CEO/Founder: Cheylaina Fultz
@HBCULegacyFashion
@HBCULegacyFashion
contact@hbculegacyfashion.com
www.hbculegacyfashion.com

HBCU Pride Nation
CEO/Founder: Travis Jackson
@HBCUpridenation
@HBCU Pride Nation
travispjackson@gmail.com

HBCU Pulse
CEO/Founder: Randall Barnes
@HBCUpulse
@thehbcupulse
www.hbcupulse.com

HBCU Recruitment Center

CEO/Founder:
  Dr. Tomisha Brock-Price
3925 N. Martin Luther King Jr. Drive
Ste 209
North Las Vegas, NV 89032
✉ hbcurecruitmentcenter@gmail.com
🌐 www.hbcurecruitmentcenter.org

HBCU Times

CEO/Founders: David Staten, Ph. &
Bridget Hollis Staten, Ph.D
📷 @HBCU_times8892
f @HBCU Times
✉ hbcutimes@gmail.com

HBCU Wall Street

CEO/Founders:
  Torrence Reed & Jamerus Peyton
f @HBCU Wall Street
✉ info@hbcuwallstreet.com

H.E.R. Story Podcast

H.E.R. Story with J. Jamison
CEO/Founder: Janea Jamison
📷 @herstory _podcast
#Herstorymovement

Hidden Colours

CEO/Founder: Jahlil Witt
✉ mr.jahlilwitt@gmail.com

Hitt Squad Ent

CEO/Founder: Anthony Adighibe
🌐 www.hittsquadent.com

Holistic Practitioners

CEO/Founder: Tianna Bynum

f @Tianna Bynum

✉ tpb33@georgetown.edu

The Hookah Bull, LLC

"An Elite Mobile Hookah Service"

Owner/Operator: Roy Ector II

☎ 301-404-9735

✉ roy.ector@thehookahbull.com

www www.thehookahbull.com

ICG Marriage & Family Therapy

CEO/Founders:

Jabari & Stephanie Walthour

@thedopesextherapist

✉ stephanie@intimacycenterga.com

www www.intimacycenterga.com

iGive

CEO/Founder: Jessica Davis

✉ igiveglobal1@gmail.com

Johnson Capital

CEO/Founder: Marcus Johnson

@marcusdiontej

✉ marcus@johnsoncap.com

The Jones Journey Project

CEO/Founder: Ebonee Jones

@thejonesjourneyproject

Journee Enterprises
CEO/Founder: Fred Whit
@ @frederickwjr
f @Fred Whit
✉ frederickwjr@yahoo.com

J.Robins CPA, LLC
CEO/Founder: Joseph Robins
@ @robinscpa
f @jrobinscpa
9800 Line Hwy., Ste. 261
Baton Rouge, LA 70816
☎ 225-650-7306
✉ info@jrobinscpa.com
www www.jrobinscpa.com

Kelly Collaborative Medicine
CEO/Founder: Dr. Kathyrn Kelly
10801 Lockwood Dr., Ste. 160
Silver Spring, MD 20901
☎ 301-298-1040
www www.kellymedicinemd.com

K.Y. Turner Law Firm, PLLC
CEO/Founder: Khanay Turner, Esq.
✉ khanay.turner@icloud.com

The Lab Personal and Professional Development Center, LLC
CEO/Founder: Ebony Gourrier
www www.thelabppd.com

The Lady BUGS
CEO/Founder: Tatiana Tinsley Dorsey
@ @theladybugsoffical
f @HBCU Times
✉ ladybugs_HQ@googlegroups.com

LEMM Media Group

CEO/Founder: Cremel Nakia Burney

@cremel_the_creator

cremelburney@gmail.com

Like Minds Dine Productions

CEO/Founder: Kristin J. Meyers

tokristinmeyers@gmail.com

Little Publishing, LLC

CEO/Founder: Dr. Ashley Little

@_ashleyalittle

@DrAshley Little

info@ashleyalittle.com

www.ashleylittleenterprises.com

Swing Into Their Dreams Foundation

Co-Founders: Pamela Parker and
Lynn Demmons

swingintotheirdreams@gmail.com

www.swingintotheirdreams.com

LK Productions

CEO/Founder: Larry King

@lk_rrproduction

@Larry King

lkproduction@yahoo.com

Lou's BluBooks

CEO/Founder: Louis D. Roberts

202-560-7368

www.lousblubooks.com

Lynch Law, PLLC

CEO/Founder: Chance D. Lynch, Esq.

1015A Roanoke Ave., Ste. A

Roanoke Rapids, NC 27870

☎ 252-535-1251

MaccBoyz Entertainment

CEO/Founder: Willie Macc

@WillieMacc

www.williemacc.com

The Marching Force

700 Emancipation Dr.

Hampton, VA 23668

www.supportthematchingforce.com

themarchingpodcast.com

The Marching Podcast

CEO/Founder: Joseph Beard

marchingpodcast@gmail.com

www.themarchingpodcast.com

Marching Sport

CEO/Founder: Gerard Howard

gerardhoward@gmail.com

McKallen Medical

CEO/Founder: Sade Stephenson,
MSN, RN, AGACNP-BC

9253 Hermosa Ave., Ste. B

Rancho Cucamonga, CA 91730

☎ 747-225-6776

mckallenmedical@gmail.com

www.mckallenmedicaltraining.com

Minority Cannabis Business Association

President: Shanita Penny

📘 @MCBA.Org

🐦 @MinCannBusAssoc

in @Minority Cannabis Business Association

📟 202-681-2889

✉ info@minoritycannabis.org

🌐 www.minoritycannabis.org

Mills Academy

CEO/Founder: Airneica Mills

📟 662-822-6976

✉ millsacademy1@gmail.com

MilRo Entertainment

CEO/Founder: Chevis Anderson

✉ milrosplace@yahoo.com

MMarie Event Planning & Logistics

CEO/Founder: Megan Clay

✉ meganmclay08@gmail.com

Mr. Anthony

CEO/Founder: Anthony Adighibe

✉ mr_anthony83@yahoo.com

Music GreekΣ, Inc.

CEO/Founder: Jeremiah Johnson

📟 470-615-9567

✉ musicgreeks@gmail.com

🌐 www.musicgreeks.com

NC Dance District

CEO/Founder: Dr. Kellye Worth Hall

@ @divadoc5

f @Kellye Worth Hall

✉ delta906@gmail.com

Never2Fly2Pray

CEO/Founder: Jeffrey Lee Sawyer

@ @never2fly2pray

f @Jeffrey Lee

✉ htdogwtr@yahoo.com

NXLevel Travel (NXLTRVL)

CEO: Hercules Conway

@ @herc3k

f @Hercules Conway

COO: Newton Dennis

@ @nxlevel

f @Newton Dennis

✉ info@nxleveltravel.com

www www.nxleveltravel.com

Original Garments: Clothing Brand

CEO/Founder: Dr. Darrius Brooks

@ @original.garments

www *Coming Soon* (DM to purchase)

OEDM Group

CEO/Principal Owner: Justin Blake

@ @oedmgroup.com

✉ contact@oedmgroup.com

www www.oedmgroup.com

PacketStealer Gaming

CEO/Founder: David Matthews

✉ packetstealer@outlook.com

The Perfect Glow

CEO/Founder: Berrie Russell

✉ berrierussell@gmail.com

www www.tpglow.com

The Phoenix Professional Network

CEO/Founder: DJavon Alston

@thephoenixnetwork757

@DJavon Alston

✉ thephoenixnetwork757@gmail.com

PILAR
— WASHINGTON DC —

PILAR

Co-Owner: Nate Perry

@barpilar

✉ nate@pilardc.com

Props Enterprises, LLC

CEO/Founders: Clarence & Keyanda Satchell

✉ foreversatchell@gmail.com

Put Up Resultz

CEO/Founder: Kasheef Wyzard

@PutUpResultz

www www.putupresultz.com

Queen Series
CEO/Founder: Randall Barnes
✉ aqueenseries@gmail.com

Raggedi Luxury Durags
CEO/Founder: Chasmin Jenkins
✉ chasminjenkins@gmail.com

Reach Higher
CEO/Founder: Dr. Kesha Reed
✉ info@keshareed.com

**Reed Williams,
A Professional Law Corporation**
CEO/Founder:
   Donald R. Williams, Jr., Esq.
9343 Tech Center Drive, Suite 165
Sacramento, CA 95826
☎ 916-281-9337
🌐 www.reedwilliamslaw.com

Regal PhotoBooth
CEO/Founder: Kaleena Clarkson
✉ kaleenajp@gmail.com

Reid Creative Solutions, LLC
CEO/Founder: Aja Reid
☎ 919-822-2892
✉ info@reidcreativesolutions.com
🌐 www.reidcreativesolutions.com

Rising Stars 3lite Cheer, Dance and Tumbling
CEO/Founders:
 Dr. Ke'Shawn Roberts and
 Ke'Shone Roberts
Central Texas
504-316-9325

SC DJ WORM 803
CEO/Founder: Jamie Brunson
@SCDJWORM803
@SC DJ Worm 803
@SCDJWORM803
@SC DJ Worm 803
scdjworm803@gmail.com
www.scdjworm803.com

Sassy Suga Lip Service
info@sassysuga.com
www.sassysuga.com

Seedlinks Behavior Management
CEO/Founder: Ryan L. Williams
1533 Marshall Street
Shreveport, LA 71101
318-626-5597

Say Yes, LLC
CEO/Founder: Porscha Lee Taylor
@sayyesplanners
info@sayyescareer.com
www.sayyesplanners.com

Shani L., Relationship Enthusiast
CEO/Founder: Shani L.Farmer
@shanilrelationshipenthusiast
info@shanilfarmer.com
www.shanilfarmer.com

She Is Magazine

CEO/Founder: Ciara Horton

@sheisemagazine

@Ciara Horton

www.ciarasheisemagazine.com

Sneaux Bidness

CEO/Founder: Delano Holmes

@sneaux_bidnessla

Shonnie Murrell

BookShonnieMurrell@gmail.com

ShonnieMurrell@gmail.com

Special Occasion

CEO/Founder: Gary Norman II

@specialoccasionlive

www.specialoccasionlive.com

The Silent Majority

CEO/Founder: Rodney Henry

757-239-1039

www.dearsummerbbq.com

Social Status PR

CEO/Founder: Ray Cunningham

@SocialStatusPR

Southern University A&M College
801 Harding Blvd.
Baton Rouge, LA 70807
225-771-4500

Southern University Alumni Federation
124 Roosevelt Steptoe Dr.
Baton Rouge, LA 70807
225-771-4200
sualumni@sualumni.org

Springbreak Watches (SPGBK)
CEO/Founder: Kwame Molden
@SPGBK
@Kwame Molden
info@springbreakwatches.com

Stamp'd Travel
CEO/Founder:
Jocelyn Hadrick Alexander
@jocehadyou
jocelyn.h.alexander@gmail.com
www.stampdtravel.com

Strategic Consulting, LLC
CEO/Founder:
Desiree' C. Cotton-Turner, Esq.
4917 S. Sherwood Forest Blvd.
Baton Rouge, LA 70817
225-371-3638

Success and Religion
CEO/Founder: Micheal Taylor
successismyreligion@gmail.com

Sugar Top Spirit & Beverage Co.

CEO/Founder: Terri White

@sugartopspirits

@sugartopspirits

tl.white412@gmail.com

www.sugartopspirits.com

SwagHer

Vice President of Sales / Marketing:
Jarmel Roberson

@swaghermagazine

jroberson@swagher.net

www.swagher.net

Tavia Botanicals

CEO/Founder: Kayonca Riggs

drkayriggs@gmail.com

TLW Photography

CEO/Founder: Taylor Whitehead

mrknowitall91@aol.com

Uplift Clothing Apparel

CEO/Founder: Jermaine Simpson

@upliftclothingapparel

www.upliftclothingapparel.com

Upward Path

CEO/Founder:
Cameron Chalmers Dupree

@upwardpathtc

contact@upwardpathtc.com

www.upwardpathtc.com

The Urban Learning & Leadership Center, Inc.

President/Co-Founder:
John W. Hodge, Ed.D

✉ jhodge@ulleschools.com

Urban Millennial Lifestyle

CEO/Founder: Nolita R. Pore

◎ @themonalita
@fitlikelita

✉ contact@themonalita.com

www www.themonalita.com

The Vernon Group Cooperative Solutions

CEO/Founder: Anthony V. Stevens

◎ @investednu

✉ info@vernongroupllc.com

Vision Tree, LLC

CEO/Founder: Dr. Jorim Reed

◎ @upwardpathtc

✉ visiontreellc@gmail.com

Vision Unlimited, LLC

CEO/Founder: Kirby Denise Wilson

◎ @Kirby_Denise_

f @Kirby Denise

✉ info@teamvisionunlimited.com

www www.teamvisionunlimited.com

VJR Real Estate

CEO/Founder: Victor Collins, Jr.

@vjrtherealtor

vic@thevjrgroup.com

Yard Talk 101

CEO/Founder: Jahliel Thurman

@YardTalk101

www.yardtalk101.com

We Are Educated, Inc.

We Are Educated, Inc.

CEO/Founder: Ayanna Spivey

@ayannaceleste

ayanna.spivey@yahoo.com

Yardopoly

CEO/Founder: Ray Cunningham

@Yardopoly

yardopoly@gmail.com

www.thegamecrafter.com
(*search: Yardopoly*)

Yard Stubs

CEO/Founder: Cremel Burney

@YardStubs

partnerships@yardstubs.com

www.yardstubs.com

Zoom Technologies, LLC

CEO/Founder: Torrence Reed

@torrencereed3

support@zoom-technologies.co